"In 1517, Martin Luther ⁖
a door to challenge the Catholic ᴄⁱ——.
years later, Dr. Roger and Karen Salstrom have posed
95 questions to Protestants that turn the tables on Luther. Covering every divisive issue from purgatory to
justification, the canon of Scripture to interpretation,
the Salstroms draw from their own experience on both
sides of the Tiber. *95 Questions for Protestants* is a timely
book to help heal the Protestant schism."

Devin Rose, author and apologist

"One of the major obstacles to evangelization is the
scandal of division among Christians. We will overcome division only through frank conversation and
friendship. This book represents a great beginning for
the conversation."

Mike Aquilina, author and EWTN host

"In this well-designed book, the Salstroms give a
contemporary Catholic response to the objections posed
by Luther five centuries ago, and the modern-day
exposition of those objections by Protestant theologians
today. The responses are clear and non-polemical — in
the sense of being conversational, not antagonistic.

"As a deep, yet easy to understand overview,
this book will be helpful for those following the
Catholic-Protestant dialogue today. It will assist Protestant theologians by giving a clear, indexed explanation
of the Catholic perspective on issues that divide us. It
will be a great resource for those in RCIA, both cate-.
chumen and catechist, and for the lay Catholic trying to

understand the faith, especially on little mentioned or understood topics such as indulgences and purgatory.

"I cannot recommend this enough to all who are responding to our Lord's prayer that his followers all may be one (John 17:21) as we enter into the second half-millennium of Catholic-Protestant dialogue."

Fr. Andrew Moore, pastor
Infant Jesus Catholic Church, Lumberton, TX

95

Questions

for

Protestants

Points to Ponder

During the 500 Year Anniversary
of the Protestant Reformation
...and Beyond

Dr. Roger Salstrom

Karen Salstrom

LEONINE PUBLISHERS
PHOENIX, ARIZONA

Cover design by James Hrkach.

Published by

Leonine Publishers LLC
Phoenix, Arizona, USA

ISBN-13: 978-1-942190-34-9
Library of Congress Control Number: 2017944405

Printed in the United States of America
10 9 8 7 6 5 4 3 2 1

Visit us online at www.leoninepublishers.com
For more information: info@leoninepublishers.com

DEDICATION

This book is dedicated to our children (Guy, Nick, Bryce, Chad, Brooke, and Elaine) and grandchildren (Nicholas Brandon Del, Rebekah, Mackenzie, Kaitlyn, Nathan, Isaiah, Athena, Aurora, Eli, and Logan). May God continue to guide you on your spiritual journeys toward fully knowing the truth.

Ultimately, this book is dedicated to the Triune God who is Father, Son, and Holy Spirit. This book is our offering of *latria* (sacrificial adoration, praise, and worship). We also extend *hyperdulia* (greatest honor) to Mary, Mother of God, who always leads her spiritual sons and daughters to her Son, Jesus Christ.

"There are not more than 100 people in the world who truly hate the Catholic Church, but there are millions who hate what they perceive to be the Catholic Church.... As a matter of fact, if we Catholics believed all the untruths and lies which were said against the Church, we probably would hate the Church a thousand times more than they do."

Venerable Archbishop Fulton Sheen

Contents

Preface

There is always a story behind the story, or, as radio broadcaster Paul Harvey put it, the rest of the story. And so it is with this book. *95 Questions for Protestants* has been a bit of an evolution.

Up until about 2011, Roger Salstrom had been a life-long Protestant. He had never given much thought to the Catholic Church as a viable home for his faith due to pre-conceived notions that Catholic beliefs were misguided. Roger's wife Karen had been raised in an Italian Roman Catholic home. Unfortunately, she lacked solid catechesis and left the Church as a young adult. During her time away, she went to Protestant churches, where she adopted some false notions about Catholic doctrine and theology. All of that changed around 2011 when they both began to research Church teachings and its history in earnest. Karen soon came back to the faith, and after several years of preparation, Roger entered the Church in 2015.

Roger, as a convert, and Karen, as a returning Catholic, began to encounter a number of well-meaning, and a few not-so-well-meaning, friends who took an adversarial stand against their decision to enter the Church. Since Roger had spent his adult life in academia, research was second-nature to him. And as one returning to the Church after more than 30 years away, Karen wanted to learn and absorb all that she had lacked in her childhood catechesis. All of this helped to lay the groundwork for compiling *95 Questions for Protestants*.

The final "brick" in the foundation came when Roger and Karen began to meet with Catholic college students attending the Protestant university where Roger worked. The students had some unique issues in that setting and desired to find a deeper understanding of their faith. Consequently, this lead to more research in preparation for teaching the students.

95 *Questions for Protestants* is in effect an epiphany and a catharsis, with the hope that it will be illuminating for those seeking truth.

Acknowledgments

There are many people to thank for their influence in how this book came to be. First, we thank our parents and grandparents who raised us with a love and respect for God.

Next, we thank the churches and parishes that nurtured us in our respective journeys. Some of our basic love for Holy Scripture came initially from Protestant churches, with the fullness of truth realized in Roman Catholicism.

We would be remiss if we did not publicly acknowledge the reason Karen returned to, and Roger entered into, the Roman Catholic Church: our son Nick Libby and his wife Lori. We appreciate the love, patience, and gentle guidance you gave for more than ten years.

We are also thankful for the Catholic university students who gave us reason to find a way to address some of the struggles they faced while attending a Protestant university.

We appreciate Immaculate Heart Radio, the first means of teaching us on our journey.

We thank the many quality Catholic theologians and apologists who have educated us through their work and inspired us to deeper thinking, including Jimmy Akin, Fr. Donald Calloway, Patrick Coffin, Scott Hahn, Donald J. Johnson, Patrick Madrid, John Martignoni, Steve Ray, Devin Rose, and Tim Staples.

Finally, in one sense we need to acknowledge Martin Luther. Although his rebellion against the papacy splintered the true Church of Jesus Christ, the timing of this book is primarily due to the 500-year anniversary of his exit from Catholicism.

Introduction

"What is Truth?"
Pontius Pilate, at the Trial of Jesus Christ
(John 18:38)

Christians believe in the God of Truth, who came to us in the Incarnation as Jesus Christ. Over the period of a few short years, he walked among the people and taught the apostles all they would need in order to go out into the world with the truth of the good news (Gospel).

But what is truth?

If it is to be complete, testimony should neither omit any portion of the truth nor distort it. There are times when the basic, simple truth is sufficient. However, in most cases the complete truth is the only way in which to have all necessary information in order to have good discernment. One example might be in a murder case. The simple truth may be that someone killed another person; however, the whole truth could be that the killer's life was being threatened by the other and in the process of defending himself, a death occurred. In this case, the mitigating circumstances would likely exonerate the one who took the life of another. For the purposes of this book, we will try to reveal the degree of truth that is demanded in a court of law: the truth, the whole truth, and nothing but the truth.

In matters of faith, revelation of complete truth is critical. Upon examining the Reformation and its premises, what if the 95 Theses really did not justify a split in the church? What if it was possible to determine that the very church against which Luther rebelled was in fact the actual church of Christ and the apostles? And what if re-evaluation might give way to reunifying the church to be as Christ intended in John 17:11? The verse states, "And now I will no longer be in the world, but they are in the world, while I am coming to you. Holy Father, keep them in your name that you have given me, so that they may be one just as we are."

October 31, 2017, marks the 500-year anniversary of the Protestant Reformation, when Martin Luther nailed a series of 95 Theses (opinions) on the door of the Castle Church in Wittenberg, Germany, on October 31, 1517. The Theses were complaints Luther had against the Catholic Church, primarily regarding the use of indulgences, papal authority, and the issue of purgatory.

Although there are 95 points and some hold the erroneous belief that these represent 95 separate issues, 40 of them directly address indulgences (several others allude to it) and 15 of the points address purgatory. Luther's single act sparked a revolution against the Christian church, a divisional splintering that continues even today. According to the *World Christian Encyclopedia*, in the year 2000 there were to date over 33,000 different denominations and church organizations in the world. Of these, approximately 9,000 were Protestant, 22,000 Independents, and approximately 3,000 other denominations (Barrett, Kurian, and Johnson, 2001), all initially sparked by Martin Luther's 95 Theses, followed by a continuous pattern of division through the years. Since the time of this publication of the *World Christian*

Encyclopedia in 2000, even more denominations have emerged.

There are those who rightly argue that the bulk of these "denominations" were a collateral effect of the Reformation movement. Each time there has been a new division, it is most often lead by a person who is dissatisfied with the church he is leaving and who believes he has a new and better way to understand Holy Scriptures. In essence, the Reformed is continually being newly reformed with each new division. However, the question arises as to just which new "reformer" has the absolute understanding of God's Word and that he has discerned it correctly. Critical to this question is the fact that many of the differences that separate and divide denominations are issues of great significance to faith and the complete understanding of Christ.

95 Questions for Protestants is not meant as an exhaustive treatment of all questions people outside the Catholic Church may have. In fact, the reader may at times in various sections find himself or herself thinking, "What about (fill in the blank)?" Excellent! The purpose of this book is to present questions for Protestants to ponder. Our goal is to offer questions, along with answers that sum up the Church's teachings from Holy Scripture, the early Church, the Church Fathers, Sacred Tradition, and Catholic catechisms. Although we are not theologians or apologists, in our research for *95 Questions* we stand on the shoulders of those who are. Their perspectives coupled with historical insights give *95 Questions for Protestants* a solid foundation for anyone who seeks truth in its fullness.

We do not necessarily anticipate that someone might be instantly convinced and thereby converted. Our hope is for contemplation by the reader. Consequently, it is our hope that reading this book will lead people to further research, and hopefully to the fullness of truth that was deposited and has remained within the Catholic Church for over 2000 years. And perhaps one day we can be the church Christ intended for us to be in John 17:11, united in a oneness that as Christ said should reflect the very relationship of the Father and the Son.

Ad Majorem Dei Gloriam...All for the Glory of God!

I

The Bible

hristianity relies upon the Word of God. The Bible is the story of salvation—God's plan of redemption through his Son, Jesus Christ. Yet since the Reformation, the Bible has become a source of division. This section addresses the Bible's history, and the significance of its canonized content.

1. Since all of Christendom agreed on the 73 canonized books of Sacred Scripture for over 1000 years, why did Martin Luther remove seven of them?

There are some who believe that the Catholic Church added seven books to the Protestant version of the Bible. Ironically, it was Martin Luther who removed the books that had been canonized and understood as correct for over 1000 years. Others recognize the seven books in question as being part of the pre-Reformation Bible, but claim they should not have been included. The Catholic Church made the final determination for the official canon of Sacred Scripture at the Synod of Hippo (AD 393) and the Councils of Carthage I and II (AD 397 and AD 419) after undergoing great scrutiny to insure their authenticity for canonization. Yet in Luther's translation, he removed the seven deuterocanonical books of the Old Testament and instead grouped them as the Apocrypha. The books in question are Tobit, Judith, Wisdom, Sirach, Baruch, and 1 & 2 Maccabees. In Luther's opinion, the books in question were not held equal to the Scriptures, but might be good reading. Since the term *apocryphal* translates as doubtful of authenticity, it was used as a means of questioning the integrity of canonized Holy Scripture. The Church of England, political in nature and begun when King Henry VIII desired an unapproved divorce, further stated that the seven books could give good example of life and instruction, but were not to be used to establish doctrine (Saunders, 1994). There is evidence that Luther also was in favor of removing several New Testament books as well: Hebrews, James, Jude, and Revelation. Fortunately, those New Testament books remained. Since many of the verses in the seven deuterocanonical books are in opposition to Martin Luther's novel theological views, he had ample reason to oppose them. Regardless of the reason, Luther removed the seven deuterocanonical books long after the officially accepted canonization had occurred.

2. If Luther's belief in *sola scriptura* (Scripture alone) was true, wouldn't he have needed a table of contents specifically given to him in Scripture in order to have changed canonized Scripture?

This question is almost circular in nature and an exercise in logic. If a person is completely true to the Bible alone concept, he must be able to prove that the Scriptures inform him of that stand. When the Bible was canonized, no actual Table of Contents existed. Since there was no guide to contents, the question was what books to include in canonization. In Mark Shea's book, *By What Authority*, he expresses an interest in the process and whom to believe in the canonization of Sacred Scriptures. He states, "But I certainly could no longer claim that I had any clear idea of how I as an individual could determine canonicity simply by praying and reading my Bible" (Shea, 2013, p. 57). After his research, he rightly concluded that God must have provided a means outside of Scripture in order to make this determination. That means was the Catholic Church, as guided by the Holy Spirit.

3. Is it true that Martin Luther opened the Bible up to the people in their own language after the Catholic Church had forbidden people from reading the Bible?

This is an underlying faulty premise: that the Catholic Church in fact forbid laity from reading the Bible. This assumption is at the root of the urban legend. In AD 1534, Martin Luther did translate the Bible into German; however, it is important to realize that his was not the first German translation. The first Gothic translation was in the 4th century, and the Catholic Church also translated it into over 20 vernacular translations of both High and Low German after the invention of the printing press. Perhaps part of the confusion is due to the fact that some vernacular versions were condemned due to bad translations and the anti-Catholic notes imbedded within them (Sippo, Donahue, Bonocore, Hugh). Even so, the availability of pre-Reformation Holy Scripture is historically evident. It is reported that beginning in the 7th century, there were many vernacular translations of Holy Scripture. In *Where We Got the Bible*, Henry Graham states: "To begin far back, we have a copy of the work of Caedmon, a monk of Whitby, at the end of the 7th century, consisting of great portions of the Bible in the common tongue" (Graham, 1997, p. 70). Graham goes on to say that in the 8th century there were well-known translations by Bede, a monk of Jarrow, who died while translating the Gospel of John. Also in that century are copies by Eadhelp, the Bishop of Sherborne in Saxon, which was the language understood and spoken by the Christians of that time. Soon after that was a translation of King Alfred the Great and others. He goes on to cite similar translations in the common language in AD 1066, AD 1150, and AD 1250 (Graham, 1997).

However, the primary argument stating that the Catholic Church discouraged reading the Bible centers around the Middle Ages. For the most part, the people in the Middle Ages were not literate. Interesting to note is that because of laity illiteracy, stained glass windows and sacred art were creative ways in which the Bible stories were passed down and understood by the common people. Complicating the ability to place Bibles in the hands of people was the fact that the Bible, which was originally on scrolls in the early Church, was not mass-produced. Each Bible was painstakingly hand-written prior to Gutenberg's printing press. It could take years for a monk to transcribe a single Bible. Financial constraint was another factor. The Bible, as with all books then, was expensive to produce, taking approximately 250 sheep in order to acquire the necessary vellum for the pages. Consequently, Bibles were often chained to the pews in order to make them available to all...which gave way to the urban legend that the chained Bibles were proof that the Catholic Church deliberately kept Bibles from the laity.

Consequently, the lack of widespread Bible reading was not due to Catholic oppression, as some might believe. However, after the invention of the printing press in AD 1436, Holy Scripture was published and translated into 20 German dialects, of which these were not the only dialects published. Interesting to note is that the Douay-Rheims version of the Bible was finished in AD 1610—a year before the first King James edition appeared. The Douay-Rheims was translated from the Latin Vulgate, which also had been available to anyone. Another complaint that is frequently raised is that the Vulgate was in Latin, therefore only available to people who knew Latin. However, since only the educated were able to read at that time in history, those who were educated could also read Latin (Sippo, Donahue, Bonocore, Hugh). Therefore, to say that the Church deliberately withheld the Bible from the people is false.

4. Given that prior to Martin Luther the canonized Bible was authorized and available to all Christians, is it logical to believe that God allowed wrongful canonization, which in turn would have promoted false doctrine?

The Church authoritatively began the canonization of the 73 books of the Bible in AD 397 at the Council of Carthage. Prior to this, there was no Bible. Canonization was not seriously questioned until the 1500s by Martin Luther, some of which was due to his personal and new interpretation of doctrine. To have canonized Sacred Scripture be in error for over 1000 years is to say that Christ's promise to protect the Church from the gates of Hell was in error. The Christian Church was diligent in its process, studying and reviewing the many other possible gospels and apostolic writings that were around at the time. Henry Graham in *Where We Got the Bible* speaks of approximately 50 gospels, 22 acts, and a smaller number of epistles and apocalypses (Graham,

1997, p. 21). Those writings, some from the early Church Fathers, were used in practice, but were rejected for inclusion in the final version, as they did not meet the high level of scrutiny required. It is illogical and irreverent to believe that Christ's Church would have been able to lead believers into error for over 1000 years by faulty canonization. Instead, the Holy Spirit guided the Church in order to safeguard the truths of Scripture so as not to be compromised by false teaching.

5. Did Jesus or the New Testament Gospel writers ever quote or reference the seven books that Martin Luther removed from canonized Scripture?

The short answer is "yes." In fact, from Matthew through Romans, there are over 200 verses that directly reference the seven deuterocanonical books, with even more throughout the remainder of the New Testament. This fact begs the question: Since the New Testament writers and Jesus himself found these words of Scripture valuable enough to cite, was it prudent to remove the very books Jesus and the New Testament writers referenced? Below is a selection of New Testament verses, along with the deuterocanonical verses referenced. For a more extensive list, visit JimmyAkin.com (see Suggested Reading List).

> Matthew 6:12, 14-15 — "Forgive us our debts, as we forgive our debtors; if you forgive others their transgressions, your heavenly Father will forgive you. But if you do not forgive others, neither will your heavenly father forgive your transgressions."

Sirach 28:2 – "Forgive your neighbor's injustice; then when you pray, your own sins will be forgiven."

Luke 1:17 (describing John the Baptist) – "He will go before him in the spirit and power of Elijah to turn the hearts of fathers towards children and the disobedient to the understanding of the righteous, to prepare a people fit for the Lord."

Sirach 48:10 – "You are destined, it is written, in time to come, to put an end to wrath before the day of the Lord, to turn back the hearts of fathers towards their sons, and to re-establish the tribes of Jacob."

Luke 1:28, 1:42 – "And coming to her, he said, 'Hail, favored one! The Lord is with you!'... 'Most blessed are you among women, and blessed is the fruit of your womb.'"

Judith 13:18 – "Then Uzziah said to her: 'Blessed are you, daughter, by the Most High God, above all the women of the earth; and blessed be the Lord God, the Creator of heaven and earth.'"

Luke 1:52 – "He has thrown down the rulers from their thrones, but lifted up the lowly."

Sirach 10:14 – "The thrones of the arrogant God overturns, and establishes the lowly in their stead."

Luke 12:19-20 — "I shall say to myself, 'Now as for you, you have so many good things stored up for many years, rest, eat, drink, be merry!' But God said to him, 'You fool, this night your life will be demanded of you; and the things you have prepared, to whom will they belong?'"

Sirach 11:19 — "When he says: 'I have found rest, now I will feast on my possessions,' he does not know how long it will be till he dies and leaves them to others."

Luke 18:22 — "When Jesus heard this, he said to him, 'There is still one thing left for you: sell all that you have and distribute it to the poor, and you will have treasure in heaven.'"

Sirach 29:11 — "Dispose of your treasure as the Most High commands, for that will profit you more than the gold."

John 3:12 — "If I tell you about earthly things and you do not believe, how will you believe if I tell you about heavenly things?"

Wisdom 9:16 — "Scarce do we guess the things on earth, and what is within our grasp we find with difficulty; but when things are in heaven, who can search them out?"

John 5:18 — "For this reason the Jews tried all the more to kill him, because he not only broke the Sabbath, but he also called God his own Father, making himself equal to God."

Wisdom 2:16—"He judges us debased; he holds aloof from our paths as from things impure. He calls blest the destiny of the just and boasts that God is his Father."

John 10:29—"My Father, who has given them to me, is greater than all, and no one can take them out of the Father's hand."

Wisdom 3:1—"But the souls of the just are in the hand of God, and no torment shall touch them."

Romans 2:11—"There is no partiality with God."

Sirach 35:12—"For he is a God of justice, who knows no favorites."

Romans 9:21—"Or does not the potter have a right over the clay, to make out of the same lump one vessel for a noble purpose and another for an ignoble one?"

Wisdom 15:7—"For truly the potter, laboriously working the soft earth, molds for our service each several article: both the vessels that serve for clean purposes, and their opposites, all alike; as to what shall be the use of each vessel of either class, the worker in clay is the judge."

Romans 11:24—"For who has known the mind of the Lord, or who has been his counselor?"

Wisdom 9:13 — "For what man knows God's counsel, or who can conceive what the Lord intends?"

1 Thessalonians 2:16 — "(The enemies of Christ persecute us), trying to prevent us from speaking to the Gentiles that they may be saved, thus constantly filling up the measure of their sins. But the wrath of God has finally begun to come upon them."

2 Maccabees 6:14 — "Thus, in dealing with other nations, the Lord patiently waits until they reach the full measure of their sins before he punishes them; but with us he has decided to deal differently."

James 1:13 — "No one experiencing temptation should say, 'I am being tempted by God'; for God is not subject to temptation to evil, and he himself tempts no one."

Sirach 15:11-12 — "Say not: 'It was God's doing that I fell away'; for what he hates he does not do. Say not: 'It was he who set me astray'; for he has no need of wicked man."

James 5:2-3 — "Your wealth has rotted away, your clothes have become moth-eaten, your gold and silver have corroded, and that corrosion will be a testimony against you; it will devour your flesh like a fire."

Judith 16:17 — "The Lord Almighty will requite them; in the day of judgment he will punish them: he will send fire and worms into their flesh, and they shall burn and suffer forever."

6. Was Martin Luther correct in removing books from canonized Holy Scripture?

If we agree with 2 Timothy 3:16, no changes should ever be made in Holy Scripture. Even in the book of Timothy itself there are several scriptural references to the deuterocanonical books (2 Timothy 4:8 / Wisdom 5:16; 2 Timothy 4:17 / 1 Maccabees 2:60). It was unwise for Martin Luther to remove the very books referenced. It was under his own interpretation and authority that Luther altered the Word of God. By definition, Luther's changes based upon his personal ideas should not have occurred.

7. If one accepts Martin Luther altering Holy Scripture, would it be valid if another "reformer" adds, removes, or changes other passages of the Bible under a new interpretation?

There is likely not one denomination that would authorize such tampering with God's Holy Word today. It would be unthinkable! The word that might come up in such a situation would be heresy. The irony is that Martin Luther did that very thing, altering canonized Scriptures that had already been rightly settled in ecumenical councils. If we accept Luther's reasoning to change Scripture (which is open to debate), then what is there to stop anyone else from changing the Holy Word of God now or in the future? Either the Bible is the inspired Word of God and should have remain intact since canonization, or it is not inspired and any human being can change it using some new interpretation. That is why the Catholic Church has not changed or authorized changes in Scripture from their original time of canonization.

II

The Church

his section looks at the historical Church. The information gives a picture of the early Church and her foundation as established through Christ.

8. Is there any historical evidence to show that the apostles and the early Church worshipped like the Catholic Church does today?

One way to know is to read the accounts of the early Church Fathers. In the First Apology, St. Justin Martyr gives a detailed explanation of how the Church worshipped each week:

> On the day called Sunday, all who live in cities or in the country gather together to one place, and the memoirs of the apostles or the writings of the prophets are read, as long as time permits; then, when the reader has ceased, the president verbally instructs, and exhorts to the imitation of these good things. Then we all rise together and pray, and as we before said, when our prayer is ended, bread and wine are brought, and the president in like manner offers prayers and thanksgivings, according to his ability, and the people assent, saying Amen; and there is a distribution to each and a participation of that over which thanks have been given, and to those who are absent a portion is sent by the deacons (St. Justin Martyr, Ch. 67).

This account translates directly to the order of the Catholic Mass. First, believers gather. Then there is a series of readings, ending with a Gospel reading. After that, there is a homily or sermon that explains the readings, encouraging all to imitate what's been read. Next, the congregation stands in prayer. After prayer, there is the Consecration of the bread and wine for the reception of Christ's body and blood during Communion. Prayers and thanks are then offered by the priest. At the end of the Consecration, the faithful respond together, "Amen," and the Eucharist is served. At the close of Communion, consecrated hosts are distributed to those who will bring them to the ill. One thing to consider is that in Luke 22:19, Christ commanded that we follow his example in the Last Supper in memory of him. The early Church set Sunday aside for worship in honor of the day Christ rose from the dead. Each denomination has its own method of worship; however, the Catholic Church continues to follow the model of the early Church in the Sunday Mass.

9. What or who is the rock on which Jesus built his Church, as stated in Matthew 16:18?

Jesus said, "And so I say to you, you are Peter, and upon this rock I will build my church, and the gates of the netherworld shall not prevail against it." There is much speculation on the meaning of "rock." When it is simply translated, it is easy to become confused as to the meaning of *rock*, as it's related to a root word in both Peter and rock. There has been much debate in Protestant circles to define the words to be differentiated by "little rock" and "big rock." However, true exegesis demands us to examine both definition and context, along with how such terminology was used in general, and in keeping with what is the discoverable meaning of the author. The Greek term for Peter is *Petros* (male), and the term for rock is *petra* (feminine). Protestants have an interpretation of these words meaning big rock (Peter's belief or faith in Christ) vs. little rock (Peter himself). But Jesus did not speak Greek; he spoke Aramaic. According to author David Currie:

> The insurmountable problem with the Evangelical analysis of the Greek text is that in Aramaic, the language of Jesus, there was only one word for rock (*Kepha*). The Greek text is itself a translation of the original Aramaic. There was no possibility of the original hearers being confused about Jesus' meaning. The disciples had to have heard Jesus saying, in Aramaic, "I tell you that you are Rock (*Kepha*), and on this Rock (*Kepha*) I will build my church." There is not the slightest room for any other meaning in the words Jesus originally uttered! The Church would be built on Peter as "rock", as distinguished from the other apostles there that day with him. The Aramaic word for "rock", transliterated into English, can be written *Cephas*. That this name for Peter is used elsewhere in Scripture lends further support for the Catholic understanding of this passage (see Jn 1:42; I Cor 1:12, 3:22, 4:5, 15:5; Gal 2:9-14) (Currie, 1996, p. 76).

If our own modern interpretations, with our own pre-suppositions, are imposed on a text, only eisegesis occurs. Consequently, it is not in keeping with the actual meaning, thus giving a faulty biblical interpretation.

Following proper methods of exegesis, it is evident that Jesus was commissioning St. Peter to be the earthly head of the Church after Jesus was taken up into Heaven. In this way, under councils headed up by St. Peter and papal successors, the Church would always have a visible authority to maintain orthodoxy as Christ intended in order to stave off the gates of Hell.

10. Is the Catholic Church the name of the Church that Jesus built?

It may be surprising that as early as AD 107 in documents written by St. Ignatius of Antioch, an early Church Father taught by St. John the Apostle, the Christian Church was referred to as the Catholic Church. St. Cyril of Jerusalem in the 4th century expounded on that thought, saying that the Church is called Catholic not only because it is spread throughout the world, but because it teaches completely and without defect all the doctrines which ought to come to the knowledge of men (the full deposit of truth). As many non-Catholics state, it was considered a "universal" Church, and that is the distinction of being catholic (small "c"). But it was termed Catholic because of a particular identity stemming from teachings of the early Church that connect to the Bishop of Rome, as the Diocese of Rome is the heart of the Church. However, there are many rites that make up the Catholic Church (Roman/Latin, Byzantine, Chaldean, Maronite, and other Oriental rites). Each of these rites are connected in their unity with the Vicar of Rome (i.e., Pope), who was designated from the Church's beginning as head of the visible Church on earth. Wherever there is unity with the Pope, therein lies the Church that Jesus built (Whitehead, 1996).

11. What is the "church" that will survive the gates of the netherworld in Matthew 16:18?

In Matthew 16:18, Christ not only designates St. Peter as the rock upon which the visible Church will be built on earth, but promises it will survive even the gates of the netherworld when he says, "And so I say to you, you are Peter, and upon this rock I will build my church, and the gates of the netherworld shall not prevail against it." At the time of St. Matthew's Gospel, the Church was only one Church. It was designated and demonstrated by Christ in practice, doctrine, and structure. These practices protected by a unified Church, apostolic in nature and lead by a visible head in St. Peter and his successors, ensured that the Church might continue to thrive and spread throughout the world. Therefore, the Church to which Christ refers only could logically be the one Church in existence then: the Catholic Church (refer to Question 8 which describes in the First Apology of St. Justin Martyr the celebration of Holy Mass in the early Church, as a model carried down through all centuries in Catholicism). Through study of early Church writings depicting all that was taught by the apostles, it is clear that the Catholic Church of today is in fact the same Church Jesus spoke of in Matthew 16:18.

12. Is it logical that Jesus would build a Church and let it be in error for 1500 years, only to be "corrected" by Martin Luther?

There is no indication that Jesus left the Church other than in the way he intended it to continue. This is evident when he states *he* will build his Church. By definition, he promised to personally build the Church, leaving it for the apostles to share with the world, increasing it numerically and geographically. Christ left an intact, perfect Church for the apostles to then continue under the authority and leadership of St. Peter, the visible leader on earth. Yet even though the Church was intact, the practices would need to be preserved and passed down. That has been the mandate for the Church since the time of Christ. Within the Catholic Church, those practices and doctrines have been preserved through apostolic succession and outlined in detail through writings of the early Church Fathers. Then, as heresies arose, Church councils formally defined doctrine so as to preserve it infallibly for all time. This is the method of the Church being protected from the gates of the netherworld. That is why it is unreasonable to believe God would allow the Church Christ built to remain and promote error for 1500 years.

13. If there is to be one Church, why are there so many different Protestant and non-denominational churches, each one having different interpretations of the same Scripture passages, many in serious interpretational conflict with the others?

The short answer to this is that since there is no visible, final authority in matters of faith and doctrine except within the Catholic Church (i.e., the Magisterium or teaching office of the Church consisting of the Pope and bishops), it leaves critical issues up to individual interpretation in denominationalism. Consequently, one group or even an individual may discern an important issue in a very different way from another. Obviously, this creates inherent problems for discernment. Many of these areas are significant—issues that are vital in understanding Christ and salvation. To miss the mark on some of these is to completely miss Jesus. Here are only three of those issues where there is major disagreement (Note: Many denominational church splits have occurred over issues of even less significance than these):

BAPTISM
(1 Peter 3:21 "...baptism...now saves you.")

Catholics, plus Lutherans, and Anglicans/Episcopalians, believe that baptism is not just a symbol, but it actually is part of the saving process for the forgiveness of sins. The Reformed Church uses the word sacrament, but it has a different meaning. And many denominations think of it as simply a symbol. Additionally, there are the methods and ages of recipients in conflict. If in fact baptism does save us, and some denominations believe that, this area of disagreement is huge. (See "Section X: Other Sacraments" for further understanding of baptism.)

TRANSUBSTANTIATION
(Matthew 26:26, Mark 14:22, Luke 22:19)

The Catholic Church has a complete acceptance and understanding of this doctrine of the Eucharist, basing it in part on Jesus' statements in the John 6 Bread of Life discourse...the only place in Scripture where disciples left Jesus due to this difficult teaching. Lutherans come close with their understanding of consubstantiation (Jesus' body and blood coexisting with the bread and wine). However, most Protestant denominations hold to a symbolic view of their participation in communion.

Who Christ is, and what he meant by "This is my Body, This is my Blood" is of great significance and key to understanding Salvation. (See "Section IX: The Eucharist," for further explanation.)

JUSTIFICATION
(James 2:24)

The faith, works debate has been an ongoing issue between Catholics and Protestants. In fact, James was one of the books Luther wanted to eliminate precisely due to this verse as it was troublesome in regards to his new doctrine of *sola fide*, or faith alone. Even so, Catholics, along with Methodists and some non-denominational congregations, have a similar fundamental concept that works are an important part of the process. However, the changing of terms is what began the separation and confusion. The biggest issue is the insertion of the word "alone" after "faith" in understanding the James passage. Nowhere in the original text of Holy Scripture do we find the words "faith alone" being the means for salvation. Instead we find in James 2:14-26 that not only is faith without works dead, but that we are *not* saved by faith alone. That, along with 2 Thessalonians 2:15 which implores the early Church to "...hold fast to the traditions that you were taught, either by an oral statement or by a letter of ours," gives us a deeper understanding. Even so, faith alone has become the battle cry of Protestantism, summarily and permanently separating Catholics and Protestants on this important issue. (See "Section IV: Faith Alone and Once Saved, Always Saved," for more on this.)

14. If one believes in the inerrancy of Scripture as Martin Luther did, what does the Bible say is the final authority for discerning the meaning of Scripture passages?

Outside Catholicism, the prevailing view is that Scripture is sufficient to interpret Scripture. There is an inherent problem in this view: nowhere in Scripture do we find a verse or passage that gives this very specific instruction. Instead we find that the Bible informs us of where to find the pillar and foundation of truth. In 1 Timothy 3:15, Scripture clarifies that the Church, not Scripture, is the final authority. In part this makes sense since there was no Bible for three centuries, and the Church relied on oral holy (not human) Tradition, along with the authority of St. Peter and the early bishops. This means that the Church is defined as the pillar and foundation of truth, not the Bible. This becomes problematic for denominationalism. Since there is no earthly single authority at the head of Protestantism to be the pillar and foundation, and since Bible interpretation is merely subjective, there are no clear answers that point to absolute truth. As discussed previously (Q. 13), in areas of greatest significance to salvation (ex: baptism, the Eucharist, justification), the absence of a definitive authority opens the door to a vast possibility of interpretations, many of which may inhibit the salvation process itself. The Catholic Church takes 1 Timothy 3:15 as the methodology for authority. As previously discussed (Q. 9), Christ designated this authority in the Church first to St. Peter as the Vicar of Christ, then continued through apostolic authority and passed down to subsequent vicars. The unbroken apostolic line of bishops, guided by the Holy Spirit and enhanced by the full deposit of truth maintained within the Catholic Church, continues the biblical guideline of the Church being the pillar and foundation of truth, consequently containing the proper authority for discernment.

15. Did Martin Luther, by setting himself up as a new authority on Scripture, start a process that allows for denominational or non-denominational churches to change their position on doctrine over time?

This is the slippery slope created by a lack of authority. Who is to define what is actually correct if there is no final authority? If a pastor relies on his interpretation of Holy Scripture, he has in essence made himself the pope for his church. However, each denomination (if there is dogmatism from the top) or each church (if there's autonomy) then has the ability to "authoritatively" define Scripture to fit local interpretation. Compounding the problem is when each church has a board that votes on matters. This reduces their form of Christianity to a mere democracy, certainly not what Christ intended. Truth is not fluid, and God's only authority for maintaining the Church and protecting it from the gates of Hell exists on earth as designated by Christ Himself in the Seat of Peter, with subsequent vicars after St. Peter installed to this role. This is the reason that doctrine discerned, settled, and infallibly defined in ecumenical councils is not able to be changed no matter what the political climate may be. Not even a pope is able to change defined doctrine. In contrast, many denominations have changed their strongly held doctrine in recent years, swayed by current thought rather than settled doctrine (ex: women

pastors, stand on homosexual unions, abortion, eutha-
nasia, etc.). One might actually say that, yes, denominational churches are completely justified in changing
these ideas precisely because they do not have an ultimate head that can define and settle truth on issues,
as opposed to the Catholic Church which relies on the
teaching office of the Church in the Pope and Magisterium.

16. Since the time of Martin Luther, isn't it virtually
    impossible to execute the mandate for Church dis-
    cipline (even excommunication) when it is needed?

In 1 Corinthians 5:1-5 and 1 Timothy 1:20, the Bible talks about excommunication. In the 1 Corinthians'
passage, St. Paul addresses an issue of incest, asking
that the one who "did this deed" be expelled from their
midst, delivering him to Satan. In 1 Timothy, St. Paul is
similarly strong when he states he has even handed two
believers over to Satan to be taught not to blaspheme.
The Church mechanism has always been in place, understanding that the Church was intended to be a singular entity. Excommunication was not only offered as
a possibility, but demonstrated as necessary in some
cases. However, outside of an apostolic setting, if a person is found to be in a serious sin that jeopardizes the
integrity of the Church, that person can simply go down
the street and find another church…or even start one of
their own. In effect, our scriptural mandate to discipline
or even excommunicate in order to chastise, teach, and
protect the integrity of the Church becomes impossible.
Although an individual denomination may have some
sort of mechanism in place, it does nothing to prevent

the person from moving on to another denomination, rendering the discipline null. Conversely, even today within the Catholic Church it is possible to continue the biblical practice of Church discipline because the Catholic Church exists and maintains its integrity under a single authority just as it was designed to do. There have been numerous people throughout the history of the Catholic Church who have been excommunicated, generally for issues of either spreading heresies or public figures openly causing scandal by their illicit lifestyles. Even as recently as the 21st century there have been excommunications involving priests promoting non-Catholic positions, illicit ordinations, schisms, and a nun allowing an abortion (she later reconciled and is no longer in the state of excommunication). A similar discipline that falls just short of excommunication is also provided in Canon Law, where a person who is persistent and unrepentantly causing public scandal in their sin can be refused the Sacrament of Holy Eucharist; some bishops have utilized this. It is clearly impossible to follow the biblical mandate of discipline outside the apostolic community.

17. Doesn't Martin Luther's "reformation" violate Jesus' words "upon this rock I will build my Church"?

It is difficult to support denominationalism when reading Christ's words. His Church is meant to be singular, visible, and significant. With estimates as high as over 30,000 – 40,000 denominational and community organisms worldwide now, each with conflicting interpretations and doctrines or dogma, the view of post-Reformation "Christianity" becomes a chaotic, un-connected network. Each believes theirs to be the true church, yet that is impossible. There are some who state that all denominations are connected because they agree on the "essentials"; however, they all do not agree on exactly what those essentials are, or the details of those essentials (consider the previous discussion on baptism, justification, and the Eucharist, in Question 13). God is not the God of chaos; He is the God of Truth. To support the growing number of church organizations, one must suspend the concept of God in Christ as the undeniable and unchangeable, complete Truth. Instead, we would need to believe that the many representations of Christ through each denomination's view are all correct. Such a position denies that Christ is Truth, and that he in-tended a Church unified in him. This disjointed cacoph-ony of opposing doctrines cannot be the Church Christ spoke of.

18. Did Christ intend an invisible church as denom-inationalism implies, or a visible Church, as Catholicism has been since AD 33?

We can find evidence of the early Church teaching a visible Church. Ignatius of Antioch (AD 107) stated, "Where the bishop is found, there let the people be, even as where Jesus Christ is, there is the Catholic Church." This is a clear indication that the Church was to be visi-ble and under clear authoritative leadership in the Bish-op of Rome (i.e., Pope). But even further back we know from Sacred Scripture that St. Paul taught one faith, and in the first major decision for the visible Church in the Jerusalem Council it was decided that Gentiles were to be exempted from the Mosaic Law of circumcision. By being a visible Church under authority, there can be no mistaking what the Church believes. The visible authority of the Church has created some of the most important historical outcomes...things like the dates for Christmas and Easter celebrations, canonization of Sacred Scripture, and even the calendar through Pope Gregory XIII. Even if heresies rear their ugly heads, they are publicly and authoritatively addressed under a visible Church; visibility creates unity and the faith is protected. Ecumenical councils have been and will always be the Church's transparent and visible presence. Conversely, to support an invisible church is to allow for straying from doctrine, or creating new separate doctrine. The invisible church since the Reformation has allowed for greatly divergent views in significant matters of faith, as well as the further splintering of Protestantism throughout the years.

III

Scripture vs. Scripture Plus Tradition

artin Luther's proclamation, in his speech at the Diet of Worms in AD 1521, that the Bible alone (*sola scriptura*) provides complete understanding of faith is the basis for a major division between Catholics and Protestants. The Catholic Church has consisted of a three-legged stool since the beginning in AD 33: Sacred Scripture (Bible), Sacred Tradition (holy oral Tradition), and the Magisterium (teaching body). If one leg is removed, the stool collapses. This section will show that the *sola scriptura*, one-legged stool foundation was and is counter-biblical.

19. Is Luther's concept of Bible alone (*sola scriptura*) supported by or found in Scripture?

Such a Scripture does not exist. Some Protestants point to certain Scripture verses as proof for *sola Scriptura*. For instance, in 2 Timothy 3:16 we learn that all Scripture is not only inspired by God, but is useful for teaching and training. However, it does not state that Scripture *only* should be used. Conversely, we see in Acts 2:42 that the early Church devoted themselves to the apostles' teachings (oral tradition). And in 2 Thessalonians 2:15 is a directive to hold to the traditions the apostles taught. In effect, holy Tradition is given credence as a means of knowing the faith. Those traditions (not human traditions) have been passed down from the apostles, preserved in the writings of the Church Fathers, and remain as the full deposit of truth of the Catholic Church.

20. Are there other reasons why Martin Luther's new doctrine of *sola scriptura* was illogical?

According to James Akin, there are several compelling reasons not to rely upon *sola scriptura*. He writes,

> ...*sola scriptura* presupposes (1) the existence of the printing press, (2) the universal distribution of Bibles, (3) universal literacy, (4) the universal possession of scholarly support materials, (5) the universal possession of adequate time for study, (6) universal nutrition, and (7) a universal education in a high level of critical thinking skills.
>
> Needless to say, this group of conditions was not true in the crucial early centuries of the Church, was not true through the main course of Church history, and is not even true today. The non-existence of the printing press alone means *sola scriptura* was totally unthinkable for almost three-quarters of Christian history! (Akin, 1996).

What this points to is that in order for *sola scriptura* to have even been possible, a literate, nutritionally healthy (in order to be able to concentrate) population, with time to devote to study, and a library of support materials for understanding was necessary. That simply did not exist and, as Akin points out, is even non-existent today in many areas of the world. Hence, oral tradition becomes critical to the masses in order to pass on the faith.

21. Did Jesus command the apostles to share the good news by having everyone read the Bible?

In Mark 16:15, Jesus tells the apostles to proclaim the Gospel to every creature (i.e., speak it). Then in Romans 10:17, we are told that faith comes from hearing, not reading. One needs to remember that during the time of Jesus, there was no written New Testament. There was only what had been passed down in the Jewish writings of what is now known as the Old Testament, and oral tradition had passed it down father to son prior to it ever being formally written. Jesus, the Word of God, became the new covenant as a living being who spoke truth and doctrine to the apostles...it was a new oral tradition. In fact, in John 21:25, we see that much of Christ's teaching and ministry was of such a large quantity that it was not even recorded formally. Consequently, Jesus did not command the apostles to first write the Bible, wait for it to be canonized, and then print it in indigenous languages and distribute it. That would have been ludicrous, since the bulk of society did not even read. Instead, he left us an earthly head (St. Peter), a council (the apostles), and oral tradition. This was how the apostles were to continue the faith and share the good news of Christ.

22. How does Scripture inform us that faith is to be passed down?

Scripture is very clear: the faith is passed on by both the written word, Sacred Scripture, and the spoken word, in the form of Sacred Tradition. As history shows, after Christ died and arose, the written word slowly emerged in the form of letters to the early Church. However, none of this was formally canonized until the 4th to early 5th centuries. How then did the apostles instruct converts in doctrinal truth? The Church relied upon the method in which Jewish culture passed down many things: oral tradition. Held within these orally transmitted doctrines was not only the foundation for faith in Christ, but also the practices taught by Christ to the apostles. By teaching in the oral tradition manner, coupled with letters to the various geographical areas, the apostles formulated what is considered the *full* deposit of truth, which continues within the Catholic Church today. Sacred Scripture never refers to itself as the final authority. Instead, we find a dual instruction method. One part is not complete without the other, as previously discussed in 2 Thessalonians 2:15, and also stated in 1 Corinthians 11:2, "...hold fast to the traditions, just as I handed them on to you," and 2 Timothy 2:2, "...and what you heard from me through many witnesses entrust to faithful people who will have the ability to teach others as well." The apostolic model for teaching the faith through both the written word and oral tradition is clearly outlined in Sacred Scripture.

23. Regarding Martin Luther's concept of *sola scriptura*, did the apostles and the early Church solve issues such as Gentile circumcision by reading the Bible?

The apostles could not have used the written Word of God in the New Testament, as it did not exist. Instead, the Church relied on the authority given to St. Peter in council with the established bishops in order to discern. This was an early form of the Magisterium of the Catholic Church. At the first council, the Council of Jerusalem in approximately AD 50, St. Peter and St. Paul were challenged to determine how circumcision was to be viewed in light of Christ and his teaching. In Acts 15:6, we see that the apostles and the presbyters met to discuss the issue. Although most Christians in this era were Jews and circumcision was understood to be required, Christianity's expansion and evangelization of converts from areas where circumcision was repulsive created the need for an authoritative intervention. Eventually, the practice that was associated with the Covenant of Abraham was abandoned for the New Covenant in Christ, and the circumcision of gentiles was deemed not to be required. Led by the Holy Spirit, they came to their conclusion in union with each other. Ever since that first council, subsequent councils consisting of the Vicar of Christ along with worldwide bishops have convened in order to decide upon issues of faith and morals. Statements defining doctrine are then issued in order to lead the faithful. These teachings are not necessarily "new" beliefs; they are merely officially defined for the sake of formal teaching and clarity (ex: Theotokos, or Mary as Mother of God...see Section VIII). A further explanation of how binding dogma emerges appears in the Catechism:

> The Church's magisterium exercises the authority it holds from Christ to the fullest extent when it defines dogmas, that is when it proposes, in a form obliging the Christian people to an irrevocable adherence of faith, truths contained in divine Revelation or also when it proposes, in a definitive way, truths having a necessary connection with these (CCC, 88).

The process of formally identifying and defining existing doctrine, then further defining it as dogma, continues today exactly as the apostles modeled at the Jerusalem Council.

24. Martin Luther wanted to ignore holy Tradition, but what did the early Church Fathers teach about holy Tradition?

The early Church Fathers emphasized the importance of tradition (Papias, Eusebius of Caesarea, Irenaeus, Clement of Alexandria, Origen, Cyprian of Carthage, Athanasius, Basil the Great, Epiphanius of Salamis, Augustine, John Chrysostom, Vincent of Lerins, and Pope Agatho). Epiphanius of Salamis states, "It is needful also to make use of tradition, for not everything can be gotten from sacred Scripture" (Salamis, AD 375, 61:6). According to author Dave Armstrong (2012), St. Augustine also states, "there are many things which are observed by the whole Church, and therefore are fairly held to have been enjoined by the apostles, which yet are not mentioned in their writings." Additionally, Eusebius of Caesarea wrote,

> At that time [AD 150] there flourished in the church Hegesippus, whom we know from what has gone before.... From them has come down to us in writing, the sound and orthodox faith received from tradition (Eusebius, AD 340, 4:21).

The teachings of the early Church are clear: both Scripture and holy Tradition work together for the purpose of teaching the faith.

25. Does Scripture agree with Martin Luther that Scripture is the final authority?

There are many denominations and non-denominations that believe the Bible is the final authority. However, in Acts 2:42, we see clearly that the early Christians relied upon apostolic teachings (Tradition), since the Bible had not been compiled, canonized, or even written then. As time went on, letters written by the apostles to specifically address issues helped the Church in its understanding. However, the early Church was always rich in oral tradition. For instance, in Matthew 18:15-17 we find that the Church (not the written Word) is to be the final authority in the case of sin against a brother. There is also very strong scriptural support for oral tradition in 2 Thessalonians 2:15. The believers are told, "Therefore, brothers, stand firm and hold fast to the traditions that you were taught, either by an oral statement or by a letter of ours." This verse points to the need for the Church to protect and maintain not simply written instructions, but the very words of instruction that were spoken. It clearly shows that there were traditions passed on through the apostles' teachings, and that they were both written and oral. To rely only upon the written is to miss out on the fullness of truth. This dual teaching is the essence of the Catholic Church and gives the Church its valid and final authority in matters of faith. According to 1 Timothy 3:15, it is the Church (not the Bible) that is the pillar and foundation of truth; that is where final authority lies. If one believes the Bible is the sole and final authority, this is problematic because the Bible is very clear that it is not.

26. Does Scripture support Martin Luther's concept of personal interpretation of Scripture?

There are three Scripture passages that speak about the problems with personal interpretation. First, in 2 Peter the early Church is admonished not to rely on personal interpretation. In 2 Peter 3:16, there is warning that there are concepts much too difficult to understand, and the "ignorant" are prone to distortion of all Scripture. A second passage in Acts 8:26-40 gives the account of St. Philip and the Ethiopian eunuch who was reading a passage from Isaiah. When Philip asked him if he understood what he was reading, the Ethiopian responded, "How can I, unless someone instructs me?" (v. 31). Finally 2 Peter 1:20 states, "Know this first of all, that there is no prophecy of Scripture that is a matter of personal interpretation." In all these passages, it is made clear that personal interpretation turns a person from true teaching toward distorted understanding which comes from false teachers.

A perfect example of just how daunting is the task of interpretation comes from apologist Patrick Madrid (2001) in his book, *Where is That in the Bible?* Madrid uses the example of a simple phrase: I never said you stole money. At first glance, everyone thinks he can derive the simple meaning from what is stated; however, as Madrid points out, it is not so simple to interpret the intended meaning. What exactly is meant?

> *I* never said you stole money (maybe someone said it), or

> I never *said* you stole money (I may have thought it), or

I never said *you* stole money (perhaps I said it was another person), or

I never said you *stole* money (you may have borrowed it), or

I never said you stole *money* (maybe it was jewelry)

Upon examination, it isn't quite as simple as it first seemed. If understanding a phrase as plain as this can create a dilemma for discernment, how much more so in the case of Sacred Scripture.

Up until the Protestant Reformation, the Church followed the continuous model of apostolic succession and guidance, as established by Christ, in order to avoid misinterpretations that would lead the people astray. Personal interpretation is at the heart of the abundance of heresies the Church has needed to address over the centuries, requiring councils to be held in order to correct those unorthodox interpretations.

How does that play out in post-Reformation times? Although there are more than 33,000 denominations since Luther's day (some of which split off early, much to his chagrin), let us focus on some of the more established ones: Southern Baptists, Presbyterians, Episcopalians, and Lutherans. Although each claims Christianity and biblical authority, each views certain Scripture passages with a different interpretation. But don't stop there. Each of those denominations is then divided into a multitude of individual churches. Each pastor may have their own "tweak" on a passage that is slightly different than another of his denominational cohort pastors. Then if carried out further, each church has several Bible studies, many lead by laypeople. As they hold discussions within a given study, the layperson may have a subtle twist. Then, in keeping with the emphasis that God speaks to each person individually through the Holy Spirit, the leader allows for people to discuss their own interpretation, as seen through their eyes (eisegesis). (Note: Yes, Catholics also believe in the guidance of the Holy Spirit; however, such nudging toward personal growth are not what we are discussing here.) Understandably, any number of interpretations is then possible, creating a greater opportunity for heresy. Is there one Truth or many truths? Within the Catholic Church, apostolic succession, the Seat of Peter, the Magisterium, and Church councils have guarded God's intended truth of Sacred Scripture and doctrine or dogma. There is an inherent danger in allowing each person to be his own authority for interpretation, and this type of error is warned against in 2 Peter 3:15-17.

> And consider the patience of our Lord as salvation, as our beloved brother Paul, according to the wisdom given to him, also wrote to you, speaking of these things as he does in all his letters. In them there are some things hard to understand that the ignorant and unstable distort to their own destruction, just as they do the other Scriptures. Therefore, beloved, since you are forewarned, be on your guard not to be led into the error of the unprincipled and to fall from your own stability. [Amen.]

Such a warning should be heeded with regards to the myriad of biblical interpretations outside of a unified visible Church.

27. If *sola scriptura* is self-evident, why do Protestants have so many (at times conflicting) commentaries explaining what the Bible means?

Perhaps one should ask how many commentaries are in complete accord with one another. The variations are limited only by the number of "authoritative" authors there might be in each generation of believers. The term "self-evident" allows each person to individualize his own personal belief or interpretation, no matter how misguided. Pope Paul VI (1965) gave instruction in his Dogmatic Constitution on Divine Revelation, *Dei Verbum*, warning that the Church remains the way to guard interpretation of the word of God:

> To search out the intention of the sacred writers, attention should be given, among other things, to "literary forms." For truth is set forth and expressed differently in texts which are variously historical, prophetic, poetic, or of other forms of discourse. The interpreter must investigate what meaning the sacred writer intended to express and actually expressed in particular circumstances by using contemporary literary forms in accordance with the situation of his own time and culture. For the correct understanding of what the sacred author wanted to assert, due attention must be paid to the customary and characteristic styles of feeling, speaking and narrating which prevailed at the time of the sacred writer, and to the patterns men normally employed at that period in their everyday dealings with one another.

But, since Holy Scripture must be read and interpreted in the sacred spirit in which it was written, no less serious attention must be given to the content and unity of the whole of Scripture if the meaning of the sacred texts is to be correctly worked out. The living tradition of the whole Church must be taken into account along with the harmony which exists between elements of the faith. It is the task of exegetes to work according to these rules toward a better understanding and explanation of the meaning of Sacred Scripture, so that through preparatory study the judgment of the Church may mature. For all of what has been said about the way of interpreting Scripture is subject finally to the judgment of the Church, which carries out the divine commission and ministry of guarding and interpreting the word of God.

Methods of interpretation vary greatly, but in the Catholic Church we find tradition to inform us, as well as Church Fathers who have guided us through their writings. We know that some of these Fathers were instructed in the faith by apostles (Ignatius of Antioch, Clement of Rome, Polycarp), so their understanding of Sacred Scripture is full of the wisdom of the apostles. Subsequent Fathers expound upon and reiterate those teachings. In their writings, we find explanation of key Scriptures with implications to the full truth of our faith (baptism, the Eucharist, justification, etc.). Those who directly passed down the faith as taught by the apostles are the best "commentators" in order to understand Holy Scripture.

IV

Faith Alone and Once Saved, Always Saved

imilar to the previous section, Martin Luther's post-Reformation stands of faith alone (*sola fide*) and once saved, always saved (*fiducia*) are unsupportable by the Bible and the writings of the early Church. This section sheds light on these issues.

28. Was Martin Luther accurate in stating that a person can be saved by faith alone?

Holy Scripture must be taken in total. Although we read in Ephesians 2:8-9 that we are saved by grace through faith as a gift from God so that no man can boast, that is not the entire story. In James 2:14 we read, "What good is it, my brothers, if someone says he has faith but does not have works? Can that faith save him?" Scripture also teaches that justification depends upon works, as stated in James 2:24: "See how a person is justified by works and not by faith alone." According to Sacred Scripture, faith alone is not sufficient if it is not evidenced by works. The complacent believer who simply basks in being saved by the grace of God, yet avoids any outward sign through works, is dead in his faith. Action through works is the evidence of salvation. Justification is a process, not a single event at one point in time. Thus, the needed tension between salvation and the justification process is ongoing throughout life.

29. Martin Luther believed that the Catholic Church taught salvation is earned through works. Is that really what the Catholic Church taught, or teaches now?

The Catholic Church has never taught that good works is how people earn or obtain salvation. Holy Tradition and Sacred Scripture tell us that only by God's grace are we saved. The Council of Trent further defined how faith and works operate together by declaring that (1) anyone who says man is justified by his own works without grace through Christ, and (2) anyone who states a sinner is justified by faith alone, should be excommunicated (disciplined until heretical thought is renounced). The Church has always understood the complex and compatible relationship between salvation and justification.

30. How important is it for our salvation that we do God's will?

In Matthew 7:21 it states, "Not everyone who says to me, Lord, Lord, will enter the kingdom of heaven, but only the one who does the will of my Father in heaven." The implication of being saved by faith alone would mean that everyone who calls out to the Lord is saved, but this verse shows it not to be true. We are complex creatures fashioned after God, with body, mind and spirit. A person who says with his lips that he claims Christ as Lord yet consistently refuses to honor God by doing his will is displaying only faith, rather than the will of the Father as Jesus instructs. Christ in the Gospel of St. Matthew is clear that such a person will not enter God's kingdom. Faith alone is not consistent with Christ's teaching in this verse.

31. If one believes Martin Luther that we are saved by faith alone (*sola fide*), why does St. Paul in Philippians 2:12 call us to work out our salvation with fear and trembling?

Catholic discernment of Philippians 2:12 and its implications has been misquoted to mean that we believe we are *earning* our salvation. That is inaccurate. In a piece by James Akin, "Salvation Past, Present, and Future," he explains how salvation is a process "...*which begins when a person becomes a Christian, which continues through the rest of his life, and which concludes on the Last Day.*" This view is based in part upon scriptural verb tenses that speak of salvation in the past "...you *have been* saved..." (Ephesians 2:8); present "...as you *attain* the goal..." (1 Peter 1:8-9), "...*work out* your salvation..." (Philippians 2:12); and in the future, "And *do* this...because our salvation *is* nearer now than we first believed"(Romans 13:11), "the work of each *will come* to light for the Day *will disclose* it" (1 Corinthians 3:15), "... so that his spirit *may be saved* on the day of the Lord" (1 Corinthians 5:5). The concept of fear and trembling is common to the Old Testament, and implies how serious is our service to God and in gaining wisdom: "The fear of the Lord is the beginning of wisdom" (Psalms 111:10); "Happy are those who always fear" (Proverbs 28:14); "Serve the Lord with fear; exult with trembling..." (Psalms 2:11).

Holy Scripture further teaches that final determination of salvation depends on the state of one's soul at death, "But the one who perseveres to the end will be saved" (Matthew 24:13), and when Jesus tells us when we do our charitable acts, we do them to him, he concludes with, "Then he will say to those on his left, 'Depart from me, you accursed, into the eternal fire prepared for the devil and his angels...and these will go off to eternal punishment, but the righteous to eternal life'" (Matthew 25:41-46). Hence, our participation in service to God all the way to the end is how we work out our salvation. We are encouraged to press on to the goal (Philippians 3:14). Should we give up the race, we are then no longer "working out" our salvation, thus opening ourselves to an unprepared soul upon death. Jesus in Matthew 10:22 says, "You will be hated by all because of my name, but whoever endures to the end will be saved." The phrase "to the end" has implications. To merely believe in Jesus is not an assurance of being saved in the end, as this verse shows. Our endurance to the end is necessary. It involves the performance of the many corporal and spiritual acts of mercy and withstanding persecutions throughout our lives. A saving faith is one that perseveres. If we were only meant to accept Christ once, and at that specific point we were assured of salvation regardless of what we do or say throughout our lives, then Jesus would not have needed to point out to us to endure all the way to the end for our salvation. The preponderance of instruction in the New Testament, both from Jesus and the New Testament writers, easily dispels the notion of *sola fide* as the means to salvation and supports the Catholic view of working out our salvation with fear and trembling, as St. Paul instructs us.

32. Where in Holy Scripture do you find Martin
Luther's concept of "faith alone"?

The only place the term "faith alone" appears is in
James 2:24. Ironically, St. James admonishes us in the
verse that we are not to be justified by faith alone, but by
our works. The confusion began to arise when Martin
Luther in his revision of Sacred Scripture added the word
"alone" (*allein*, in German) to Romans 3:28. That word
was never in original manuscripts and has since been
eliminated from most translations. Even so, the concept
of faith alone (*sola fide*) has remained. It is inconsistent
that a person claims the full, sole authority of Scripture,
yet denies the instruction of James 2:24. St. James makes
it even more clear by describing a "dead" type of faith
which has no works, in James 2:17. If we deny these
two verses, we are discounting the importance of the
complete canonized Word of God. And we know from
2 Timothy 3:16 that *all* Scripture is inspired by God and
is useful. Christianity is not meant to be a smorgasbord,
where we pick and choose only the verses we find palat-
able, adding, eliminating, or minimizing those we deem
not so tasty and which do not support a preconceived
notion. Martin Luther's new doctrine of "faith alone"
fits this change he made to Sacred Scripture, and which
continues to be promoted in Protestant circles.

33. Where in the Bible is the Protestant formula for salvation of accepting Jesus as "personal Lord and Savior"?

In some Protestant doctrines, the decision to accept Jesus as one's personal Lord and Savior generally means they are instantly a saved Christian and "born again," with no further requirements in the process. However, there is no place in Holy Scripture where we find the formula of accepting Jesus as personal Lord and Savior in order to be saved. Many denominations follow this "tradition," but it is not in Holy Scripture. The Catholic Church maintains that salvation is a process. According to Holy Scripture, the salvation process begins with baptism (1 Peter 3:21) and continues throughout life as we endure to the end (Matthew 24:12-13). Our inheritance of salvation is then kept for us in Heaven, to be revealed in the end (1 Peter 1:3-5) (Thigpen, 2007). That being said, we need to be clear that the Catholic Church by its very existence and evangelization throughout history has consistently offered Christ as Lord and Savior to the whole world, as Christ desired. Catholics are given many moments within each Mass to receive anew the invitation from Christ, culminating in receiving him in the Holy Eucharist. In fact, as Section IX on the Eucharist reveals, to know Christ fully is to partake of his body and blood. That is the most intimate and public acceptance of Christ as Lord and Savior there can be.

34. Is the Protestant doctrine of "once saved, always saved" in the Bible?

The primary place given for supporting this belief is John 3:15-18, but "once saved, always saved" is not true to the passage. Here Jesus lays the foundation by which eternal life is offered. The first stone in that foundation is a belief in Christ. However, Jesus does not state that the salvation cannot be lost or that nothing else should occur in the person's walk with him. Sacred Scripture is the complete story of salvation, so to reduce the process to one concept or verse is dangerous and leads to missing the whole picture. There are numerous passages that show that one can lose his salvation. Romans 11:17-23 (parable of the branches) describes how it is possible to lose salvation, and also to regain it. Branches that once were part of the tree are described to have been broken off. But in verse 23 we are told that if "...they do not remain in unbelief, will be grafted in, for God is able to graft them in again." We also see this in the story of the Prodigal Son in Luke 15. The son was saved in the love of his family, lost by his actions that separated him from his family and father, and then saved again through his repentance and forgiveness given by his loving father. Then in 1 Timothy 5:8, it states that, "If anyone does not provide for his relatives and especially for his immediate family, he has denied the faith and is worse than an unbeliever." Again, this verse shows how a person who is not living his faith properly is considered worse off than even an unbeliever who has no salvation. This shows a loss of salvation, rather than "once saved, always saved." Finally, James 5:19-20 states, "My brothers, if anyone among you should stray from the truth and someone bring him back, he should know that whoever brings back a sinner from the error of his way will save his soul from death and will cover a multitude of sins." This passage indicates that a sinning brother in the Lord can have his soul "saved" by someone bringing him back from the path to death. In other words, a Christian can quite possibly move away from the path to life by sinning, thus putting his soul in jeopardy of "death," a euphemism for Hell. Even though this person obviously is a Christian brother (i.e., has faith), straying into the path of sin creates a possibility with grave consequences. In some forms of Protestantism, this type of person is said to be "backsliding." Although those denominations do not believe that this form of straying can separate a person from God whereby he can be eternally lost, James 5:19-20 would disagree. It also points to the need for brothers and sisters in Christ to be on the watch for those who fall into sin in order to assist them back on the path to righteousness and salvation. These passages are but a few that point to the possibility of a person losing salvation, in contrast to the faulty concept of "once saved, always saved."

35. Do the writings of the Church Fathers support Martin Luther's idea of *sola fide* (faith alone)?

There are numerous early Church writings that support the biblical truth of faith partnering with our good works for the purpose of justification and salvation. Here are just a few:

> "Seeing, therefore, that we are the portion of the Holy One, let us do all those things which pertain to holiness...being justified by

our works, and not our words" Clement of Rome, Epistle to the Corinthians, 30 (AD 98).

"They only who fear the Lord and keep His commandments have life with God; but as to those who keep not His commandments, there is no life in them" Shepherd of Hermas, 2 Comm 7 (AD 155).

"Whoever dies in his sins, even if he profess to believe in Christ, does not truly believe in Him, and even if that which exists without works be called faith, such faith is dead in itself, as we read in the Epistle bearing the name of James" Origen, Commentary on John 19:6 (AD 232).

These writings show how the holy Tradition of the Church is active in teaching the whole truth of Christianity, and assists in the avoidance of false doctrine. *Sola fide* is rendered heretical as we read from the Fathers of the Church.

V

Brothers of Jesus

T he belief in biological, full brothers of Jesus is one that effects understanding of the Virgin Mary. Although some may see no great importance in getting this one right, if viewed incorrectly it clouds our perception of the significance of Mary, the Mother of God. The Bible is a total picture, and if we get even a small section misinterpreted, it can skew other important areas. (See Section VIII for more on Mary.)

36. Protestant tradition states that Jesus had biological brothers. Is that supported in Holy Scripture?

Understanding Sacred Scripture is a daunting task at times, and requires great care in hermeneutic methods. The problem here is in translation, coupled with applying a modern-century, English definition to a term in ancient Scripture passages. In English, when we say "brother" we mean a sibling who has the same biological parents. Yet even in English, there can be an extended definition (half-brother, step-brother, adoptive brother, or even a friend). Some of the confusion is that Jesus spoke Aramaic, not the Greek from where we derive our translation of the New Testament. The meaning of brother in Aramaic includes cousins and other close relations, as there were no words for those relations in Aramaic (Schaetzel, 2013, p. 62). In the passages used to prove biological brethren, it actually is impossible to do so. The Septuagint translates the Hebrew by the Greek word *adelphos* (brother), which is the likely misunderstanding of the translation in New Testament passages, as they are used similarly. One interesting side note is that even Martin Luther understood that Mary, the

Mother of Jesus, had no other children. There truly is not one definitive passage that reveals biological brothers. In fact, the questions that follow point to passages which indicate Jesus did not have biological brothers.

37. If one translates the word "brother" literally in Acts 1, is it possible that Jesus had about 120 brothers?

In Acts 1:14-16, it lists those present as the apostles, the women, Mary the mother of Jesus, and "his" brothers—there were 120 people counted as "brothers." And then St. Peter addressed the crowd, "my brothers." If we translate the word "brothers" in verse 14 literally, there are only a couple of conclusions. Either it is stating that Mary had 120 children, or St. Peter had that many biological brothers. This example shows that the word "brothers" as translated from the Greek should not always be translated literally as biological brothers.

38. If Jesus had brothers, shouldn't his last act on the cross have been to turn over the care of his mother, Mary, to the oldest remaining brother?

Jewish culture is strong in family commitment, including an obligation for children to care for their parents. In Jesus' time, it would have been unheard of for a remaining parent to be cared for by someone other than a biological son. If Jesus had biological brothers, he would have done the proper thing by Jewish tradition and had his "brother" care for her, not St. John. It is inconceivable that Christ, the perfect and sinless Savior who was also a Jew and lived out his Jewish faith perfectly, would have then in his very last moments insulted both his family and his Jewish upbringing by handing His mother over to one who was not even a family member. If we believe this was his last formal act, it would imply Jesus sinned. Further, there is no indication of any protest from St. James, who some Protestants claim as the "brother" of Jesus. If he were truly Christ's biological brother, placing Mary in the care of St. John would have been scandalous to St. James and the whole family. In *Navigating the Tiber* (2016), apologist Devin Rose suggests to consider,

> ...why Jesus, when he was hanging on the cross, would give his mother into the care of John the apostle, if indeed he had siblings? It makes no sense; his mother would be under the care and protection of her own children and not an unrelated friend, no matter how close John might have been to her Son.

Skeptics of Christianity have also added their own erroneous fuel to the fire in a documentary by author James Cameron of *Titanic, Aliens,* and *Avatar* fame. According to Professor Michael Barber of John Paul the Great University in Escondido, California, in a Catholic Answers Live video, "The Lost Tomb of Jesus?", Cameron took archaeologists to Jerusalem where he supposedly found Jesus' bones in a "family" tomb. However, the bulk of historical tradition and geographical evidence always points to the Church of the Holy Sepulcher in Jerusalem as the actual place of Christ's burial, where believers flock each year in pilgrimage. Barber points out that in Jesus' time there were many James, Jesus, and Miriam (Mary) names. It is not a compelling argument, nor is the expedition in question reputable. In essence, to subscribe to this new theory of James as Jesus' brother, one must first deny the understood place of Christ's burial, and that the bones prove he never rose from the dead or ascended into Heaven—both of which are huge red flags for all who follow Christ. Fortunately, the bulk of non-Catholics do not subscribe to Cameron's theory; however, these new theories tend to draw our attention away from true discernment. One needs look no further than the evidence in Holy Scripture as viewed under a solid hermeneutical lens in order to find that there is no proof that Jesus had biological brothers.

VI

Saints and Intercessory Prayer

rotestants reject the notion that there is a connection between those in Heaven (Church Triumphant), those in purgatory (Church Suffering), and those on earth (Church Militant). Catholics have always maintained that intercessory prayer is beneficial. This section explains that understanding.

39. Though Protestants reject the concept of praying to anyone but God, how can prayer to others be appropriate?

Prayer can be defined in several ways. Although its common meaning is to engage in conversation with God, it has a broader meaning. It originated in Old French from *praeir* (to ask earnestly). That word was derived from the Latin, *precari* (to entreat or ask). We have seen it used in this way in Shakespeare (pray tell, or please tell me). The problem arises when the word prayer is defined to imply worship. Although we pray when we worship, prayer itself is not worship. Since worship belongs to God alone, it is understandable that if someone erroneously equates prayer with worship, that they might then only believe prayer should only be to God. However, prayer in the greater sense is not so limited.

40. How does prayer relate to the "great cloud of witnesses" in Hebrews 12:1?

Hebrews 12:1 states, "Therefore, since we are surrounded by so great a cloud of witnesses, let us rid ourselves of every burden and sin that clings to us and persevere in running the race that lies before us." The "cloud of witnesses" includes those who have gone before us and attained their heavenly home (the Church

Triumphant). As members of the greater Body of Christ, they are by definition connected to all other members of the Body. It is evident in this passage that they are able to know our journey, and cheer us on from Heaven. These saints are those to whom we pray, asking them to intercede for us. It is in complete agreement with the concepts of each person's connection to the Body, and their interest in how we run our race.

41. Protestant doctrine does not allow for intercessory prayer by those who have passed away. Given that people often ask other people to pray for them, is it biblical to ask those who have died to pray for us?

The understanding of prayer as conversation (Question 39) is key in helping to define this answer. It is likely that not one practicing Catholic or Protestant would hesitate to ask a friend to pray for them. As stated above, once we become part of the Body of Christ and remain faithful, we are eternally connected and death does not break that connection. If we believe in the eternal life of the soul, then it is not a huge leap to believe in their ability to continue to pray for us. We know from Hebrews 12:1 that those who have gone before us cheer us on in our journey from their heavenly vantage point. Since they are already in the presence of God in the Church Triumphant, they are even better suited to continue to pray for our success than those still alive. In fact, Revelation 8:3-4 shows an angel taking the petitions of the "Holy Ones" to the throne of God. The word "holy" is translated from the word "saint" (*sanctus*, in Latin). Many Catholic apologists understand the term of holy ones used here to mean the saints who have gone before us (prayers of the saints are also stated in Revelation 5:8). And in Jeremiah 15:1, God refers to Moses and Samuel who could appear before him in intercession for the people. Finally, in 2 Maccabees 15:11-16, two deceased people, Onias and Jeremiah, were interceding for the Jews. If you define praying as conversation, even Jesus engaged in this when he talked to Moses and Elijah at the Transfiguration. The bond of the Body of Christ is unbreakable, and when one hurts, it has an effect on all. Similarly, when one rejoices, all rejoice. Since the saints who have gone before us have a valid interest in our continued success as the Church Militant on earth, they are eager to participate in uplifting, intercessory prayers on our behalf. This makes it not only possible but wise to ask for their intercessory prayers.

42. Though Catholics are often criticized for praying to saints, have those prayers ever resulted in documented miraculous healings?

Intercessory prayers to the saints for healing are ongoing in the Catholic Church, and many miracles have been attributed directly to those prayers. These healings have perplexed the medical community for years. What is noteworthy is that the process for recognizing a miracle is not simple, and must be well documented. For instance, there were several steps or stages in the process for a miracle to be confirmed at Lourdes, where the Blessed Mother Mary appeared to Bernadette Soubirous in 1858. Similar documentation is required for all miracles within the Catholic Church. As at Lourdes, miracles verified are to have been in a hopeless case with no expected cure, and the unexpected cure cannot be due to any other intervention. The exceptional character of the miraculous cure is examined against all present scientific knowledge. In the end, there should be no other medical explanation for the cure. There have been 69 such cures since the appearance of the Virgin Mary at Lourdes, with the most recent in 2013. However, Lourdes is not the only place of miracles, nor is St. Bernadette the only saint whose intercessions are attributed to miraculous cures. With such a preponderance of miraculous cures documented by modern medicine, it is hard to discount their authenticity. One thing to keep in mind is that the Catholic Church in no way promotes the idea that saints heal people. This again is an urban legend, and has been the cause of great misunderstanding by Protestants. According to Catholic teaching, healing instead is always a gift from God, in union with prayers offered by the saints we have petitioned to intercede for us.

VII

Statues, Images, and Relics

imilar to Section VI, the use of statues, images, and relics in the Catholic Church have given way to great misconceptions of how the Church views them. These next questions should help clear up such wrong understanding.

43. Does the Bible support the Catholic practice of the use of relics?

A relic is generally some portion of the body of a saint (bones, hair) or a piece of their clothing, or an object that's been touched to the tomb of a saint that is held in reverence. Relics were used in the Old Testament (2 Kings 13:21) where a dead man was thrown on the bones of Elisha and the dead man came to life. Also, we see relics used in the New Testament (Matthew 9:20-22, Acts 5:14-16, Acts 19:11-12) to either heal people or raise them from the dead. The practice was continued in the early Church. A Catholic Answers tract, "Relics" (2004), describes the account of Polycarp's martyrdom (AD 156):

> We took up his bones, which are more valuable than precious stones and finer than refined gold, and laid them in a suitable place, where the Lord will permit us to gather ourselves together, as we are able, in gladness and joy and to celebrate the birthday of his martyrdom.

Anti-Catholic historian Adoph Harnack reported:

> ...[N]o Church doctor of repute restricted it. All of them rather, even the Cappadocians, countenanced it. The numerous miracles

which were wrought by bones and relics seemed to confirm their worship. The Church therefore would not give up the practice, although a violent attack was made upon it by a few cultured heathens and besides by the Manichaeans (Catholic Answers, 2004, Relics).

One of the most interesting stories of post-resurrection relics involved Emperor Constantine's mother St. Helena, of whom ancient historian Eusebius has written. At the age of 80, she made a pilgrimage to the Holy Land to look for relics for the Church. She supervised the demolition of a pagan temple on the site of Jesus' tomb near Calvary, where she found three crosses. Wanting to be certain of the correct cross of Christ, St. Helena decided to bring a woman dying from a terminal disease to the site. The woman was asked to touch the crosses, one by one. Upon touching one of the crosses, she was instantly healed. That occurrence clearly identified it as the true cross of Christ. Later, St. Cyril of Jerusalem also gave testimony in a letter to the Emperor Constantius (Constantine's son and successor). St. Ambrose spoke of how when St. Helena found the Cross, she worshipped not the wood, but Christ the King. This points to the proper use of relics. They are useful and can be venerated or honored, but only God deserves our worship. Relics are not objects of magical power, but instead sacramentals, which point believers to worship God in thanksgiving.

44. Is Protestant criticism of the use of statues, icons, and images biblically justified?

In the Old Testament, God commanded that images be made with respect to the Ark of the Covenant, the Tabernacle, a seraph used for Moses to heal the people (Exodus 25:18-22, 26:1, 31 and Numbers 21:8-9), and statues were made in the building of Solomon's temple (1 Kings 6). If somehow we denounce the use of images and statues, think about the use of images in your own home (photographs). Also think of the countless historical statues people flock to (Abraham Lincoln in the Lincoln Memorial). The confusion arises when reading the Ten Commandments, where we are told not to make and worship graven images. Nowhere in Catholic doctrine are we told to worship any statues, images, or icons. The word is "venerate," which means to honor. Unfortunately, those outside Catholicism have inaccurately judged veneration to represent worship, but Catholic theology tells us that God alone receives worship, though saints are honored for their exemplary lives. Keep in mind that even non-Catholics will set out nativities (statues) in their homes and yards as a means of honoring Christ and the Holy Family; they provide a visual focus to bring to mind our Lord and his birth. Images have always been a part of the Church, useful in focused prayer and as teaching tools (Stations of the Cross, stained glass depicting biblical stories, etc.). Christ himself was incarnate as the image of God (Greek, *ikon*). It is only when an image is graven, as in animal worship, or if we use images in illicit ways by worshipping them that we stray from God's intended purpose of icons, statues, and images within the Church.

VIII

Mary as Theotokos, Mother of God

atholic dogmas related to the Virgin Mary are difficult for most Protestants to understand. Ironically, Martin Luther's Mariology was similar to that of Roman Catholicism. He believed in her Immaculate Conception and perpetual virginity, as well as being Theotokos (Mother of God), and referred to her as the Queen of Heaven. Calvin's views were similar. Similarly, regarding Mary's perpetual virginity, other prominent reformers and founders of denominations agreed (Zwingli, early reformer; John Wesley, Anglican who founded Methodism; and Hugh Latimer, Anglican). However, in subsequent church divisions, a great number of the new denominations rejected any Mariology. This section will address Catholic historic understanding of the Virgin Mary.

45. Do Protestants ever honor special people or recognize their contribution to the work of Jesus Christ?

People in our lives and in the public realm are often given special honor. In families, some relatives are greatly honored for their wisdom and influence, such as grandparents, or special aunts or uncles. Other people who have assisted us in our own spiritual journey have a place of honor in our hearts. That might include a youth pastor or catechism teacher. In the public arena, people are honored for their contribution in their field. Public figures might include Billy Graham, Mother Teresa, and Rick Warren. It is common to show special recognition for their contribution, even once they have passed away. For instance, our country celebrates Dr. Martin Luther King Jr. Some families have times of remembrance, or an empty seat at the table for a deceased loved one. In a similar way, Mary, Mother of Jesus and a perfect example of saying "yes" to God, certainly fits into this category of those who deserve honor.

46. Are there early Church teachings that support a place of special honor to Mary?

The Angel Gabriel stated to Mary that she was "highly favored." Of such significance was the greeting that deeply troubled Mary (Luke 1:28-30). From the earliest times, the Church always understood Mary's significance and place of honor. Consequently, several Church councils reiterated and formally defined Mary's role in the Church. At the Council of Ephesus (AD 431), Second Council of Constantinople (AD 553), the First Lateran Council (AD 649), then ratified by the Third Council of Constantinople (AD 680-681), Mary's holiness, ever-virgin status, and Immaculate Conception were defined. Even post-Reformation, Martin Luther continued to subscribe to these well-founded truths.

47. Was the Virgin Mary actually sinless, as Catholics claim?

Ask Christians whether or not all humans sin and, therefore, are not perfect and in need of a Savior and the resounding "yes" will ring out around the world. Yet the Catholic Church teaches that Mary was set apart as sinless in anticipation of the Incarnation of Christ through her Immaculate Conception. The Catholic Answers tract, "Immaculate Conception and Assumption" (2004), gives an understanding of the process. The tract explains that the term immaculate conception is sometimes mistaken for Christ being conceived in Mary's womb, since there was no human father. Some others believe it means Mary was conceived like Jesus was, by the power of the Holy Spirit. Both are inaccurate. It actually means that Mary was conceived without original sin or any of its effects by the "merits" of Jesus. There is a distinctly sound reason for this miraculous act regarding Mary's conception. Christ, who is pure and completely without sin, was to remain for nine months in Mary's womb. If she had not been preserved in this way, he would have been conceived in a vessel stained by original sin, which is unthinkable. The vessel for his fetal development was pure and unblemished, as he also remained without the stain of original sin. Another testimony to Mary's lack of sin is found in the greeting from the angel at the annunciation in Luke 1:28: "Hail, full of grace, the Lord is with you." The Catholic Answers tract further explains that the Greek word *kecharitomene* represents the proper name of the person being addressed, and consequently expresses an inherent quality. The tract goes on to inform that more recent translations replace "full of grace" with "highly favored daughter":

> Mary was indeed a highly favored daughter of God, but the Greek implies more than that (and it never mentions the word for "daughter"). The grace given to Mary is at once permanent and of a unique kind. *Kecharitomene* is a perfect passive participle of *charitoo*, meaning "to fill or endow with grace." Since this term is in the perfect tense, it indicates a perfection of grace that is both intensive and extensive. So, the grace Mary enjoyed was

not a result of the angel's visit, and was only as "full" or strong or complete as possible at any given time, but it extended over the whole of her life, from conception onward. She was in a state of sanctifying grace from the first moment of her existence to have been called, "full of grace."

One other point is that many theologians outside the Church will testify to the need for the virgin birth in order to separate God from the sin of Adam. However, unless Mary was without sin, the sin of Adam would have remained within her, rendering her to be an unpure vessel. Mary's sinless quality was present in many of the early Church Fathers' writings. In his book *Meet Your Mother* (Miravalle, 2014), Mark Miravalle writes,

Church Fathers from the early centuries compared Mary to Eve's state of created purity and innocence. In other words, Mary was as Eve was before her participation in the Original Sin with Adam and her resulting fall from grace. ... Church Father St. Ambrose taught in the late 300s that Mary was "altogether without the stain of sin." By the sixth century, she was called "Immaculate"; and by the ninth century, Mary was understood to have been "conceived by a sanctifying action." This is really remarkable, since the common biological teachings of the day did not even universally accept that human life begins at conception until several centuries later!

Coupled with the many popes and other Church Fathers' writings, Mary's Immaculate Conception seems consistently understood and supported. Moreover, there is a mountain of evidence that even Martin Luther retained his Mariology, including a belief in the Immaculate Conception, according to Martin Luther's personal Prayer Book (1522).

Although those outside of Catholic and Orthodox teaching point to Romans 3:23 as a proof-text for Mary to be included in "all" who have sinned, if they acknowledge an exception to that rule for Christ, there is a good case for such an exception to have been extended to the one who bore him, the Virgin Mary.

48. Is there scriptural basis for showing Mary special honor?

Elizabeth stated to Mary, "Blessed are you among women and blessed is the child you will bear" (Luke 1:42). Queen Esther is considered a prefigure of Mary, and Esther was beloved "beyond all women," adorned with a diadem and royal crown, and made queen, surpassing all women. The angel's words of Mary being blessed among women was a statement even more honoring, and not one other biblical person was given that high a praise. Elizabeth also calls Mary "the mother of my Lord" (Luke 1:43). Again, this is a title and honor no one else has. As the Mother of Christ, and thus a participator in the salvation process, Mary has been and always should be afforded a great honor. In the Catholic faith, there are distinctions of honor. The highest is *latria* (worship), which is only afforded to God. A second is *dulea* (honor), which is given to the saints who have gone before us. Finally, there is *hyperdulea* (great or special honor). This honor is specific only to Mary for her role in the salvation by giving her yes (*fiat*) to God's call on her life. One final biblical reference that points to Mary's significance is in Luke 1:44 where Elizabeth describes how it specifically was Mary's greeting that caused John the Baptist in Elizabeth's womb to leap for joy. A special grace was given John when he recognized the voice of the Mother of God, causing his joyful movement in Elizabeth. Holy Scripture clearly shows that Mary is deserving of *hyperdulia*, and holy Tradition shows it given to Mary from the earliest times.

One last point outside of Scripture to consider is the biological phenomenon of mother-child cell exchange during pregnancy. This process is described in *Under the Mantle* (Calloway, 2013). When a woman is pregnant, cells migrate between mother and child in a process known as *fetomaternal microchimerism*, and the exchanged cells remain within each of them for life. In the case of Jesus and Mary, consider that the holy, unblemished person of Christ shared cells with his mother, Mary. To that end it follows that the perfection of Christ's very flesh remained within his mother for the rest of her life. The cell migration made Mary a perpetual vessel of Jesus. Surely, that alone awards her a place of great honor.

49. Is there valid reason for Protestants to dispute
    Mary's title of God-bearer, or Mother of God?

The terms that point to this Catholic doctrine are Theotokos, from the Greek, *Theo* (God), *tiktein* (to give birth), and *Meter Theiou* (Mother, God). These distinctions rightfully qualify her for the title "Mother of God."

When we consult Holy Scripture, there is ample reason to acknowledge she is the one who bore God Himself in the form of Jesus, the Son. In Luke 1:35, the Angel Gabriel specifically states that the child to be born will be called the Son of God. In Matthew 1:23, the child is called Immanuel, or God with us. In Galatians 4:4, we are told that God sent his Son. This and other passages are clear that Jesus was fully God and fully man. This dual identity was with him from conception. It becomes clear that giving Mary the term, "Mother of God," is not only logical, but biblically sound. If Jesus is the Son of God, and Mary is his natural mother, she is by definition the Mother of God, as the Church defined through the writings of the Church Fathers (Irenaeus, AD 189, 5:19:1), then formally at the Council of Ephesus in AD 431. Even modern Protestant theologian Karl Barth states, "The description of Mary as 'Mother of God' was and is sensible, permissible and necessary as an auxiliary Christological proposition" (Barth, 1961).

50. Does the Bible support that Mary as Mother of the King (Jesus) is to be honored?

To understand this, we need to review how God gave us models in the Old Testament of the perceived influence the Queen Mother was to have over her son. In 1 Kings 2:13-23, Queen Bathsheba (mother of Solomon) was asked by Adonijah to go to the king on his behalf because he knew the king would not refuse his mother. When Bathsheba went to Solomon, King Solomon replied, "Ask it my mother, for I will not refuse you." Normally in ancient Israel, the king would grant any reasonable request by the Queen Mother, although this particular one had political intrigue and was not granted (see 1 Kings 2:25). Another example of the Queen Mother's honor is in Jeremiah 13:18, where she is mentioned alongside the king in a place of prominence. Finally, in Proverbs 31 the Queen Mother gives advice to the king, her son. In all these examples, the Queen Mother is honored and acts in speaking for the people (intercession). This is Mary's role in the Church as intercessor for us, her children. God placed very clear examples — beautiful analogies — in the Old Testament for us to ponder as we seek to understand, know, and give honor to Mary as Mother of Christ the King.

51. To truly imitate Christ, should Protestants also show honor to Mary, his mother?

First, we need to acknowledge that Jesus, as a sinless son in a Jewish family, would have by definition followed the commandment to honor his father and mother. It would have been unheard of for any son in that culture to disrespect his mother, but in the case of Christ even more so. He was perfect and without sin. Second, if we are to truly imitate Christ, our relationship to Mary should mirror that of Jesus. Since Jesus loved and honored his mother, it is completely reasonable that we should love and honor her as well.

52. Is there proof in Scripture that Jesus gave Mary to the Church as their spiritual mother?

We already know that Mary is shown to be the Mother of God the Son. Since we as members of Christ's Church are also members of Christ's Body, Mary is our spiritual mother. We see Jesus designating Mary as such at the crucifixion when he entrusted the care of his mother Mary to John. St. John, being entrusted with

Mary's care as a "son," is a representation of the greater Church as sons and daughters. The further proof is found in Revelation 12:17-18. Chapter 12 carries on the theme from Chapter 11 of Mary as the Ark of the Covenant who, by definition, is hated and opposed by the Dragon. In these verses in Revelation 12, the Dragon then "...went off to wage war against the rest of her offspring, those who keep God's commandments and bear witness to Jesus." We, as the ones who keep God's commandments, are those offspring. Therefore, Mary is rightly known as our spiritual mother, and we her children.

53. Other than being the God-bearer, what else in Scripture points to Mary being an active participant in the salvation process?

Although Catholics understand the sufficiency of Christ for the redemption of sin, Mary played a significant role in the salvation process. She began her role by saying yes (*fiat*) to the Angel Gabriel, showing her desire to cooperate with God's plan. In doing so, not only did Mary become the first disciple of Christ, but also the first evangelist by "carrying" the Lord to the world in her womb. But bearing the Son of God did not end her part in salvation history. At the Wedding at Cana, Mary had a unique role. When the wine ran out, she unilaterally gave Jesus the word to begin his ministry by performing his first miracle, turning water to wine. Although Jesus said his time had not yet come, Mary, in her role in the salvation process, authoritatively told the servants to do whatever her Son said. This was in essence the directive to Jesus to initiate his ministry. And so began Christ's ministry, under the influence of his mother. Also, as Christ's mother, Mary shared deeply in Christ's suffering. In Luke 2:35, Simeon sought out Mary to designate her as the Mother of Sorrows, stating, "And you yourself a sword will pierce." For anyone who has lost a child, it is easy to understand the suffering of a mother. However, this phrase indicates something deep and nearly physical in Mary's suffering, a parallel participation in her Son's agony. Finally, in Acts 1:14, we find Mary actively participating with the disciples, praying in anticipation of the Holy Spirit. All of these Scriptures point to Mary's cooperation with God in the salvation process from the time of Jesus' conception to the descent of the Holy Spirit at Pentecost.

54. If Mary actually has appeared to believers as chronicled in Catholic history, isn't it important enough for Protestants to know about those events?

This may be new territory for some people. There have been numerous appearances throughout history when Mary reached out to humanity with a specific message and purpose. Some of these apparitions have not been approved by the Catholic Church, as there is a thorough process for any such apparition to find approval. That said, below are two Church-approved apparitions. It would be worthwhile for one to research more of these, but the point is that the Blessed Mother continues to reach out to her children in Christ and is deserving of recognition for her role in the Church.

Our Lady of Guadalupe

In AD 1531 on the hill of Tepeyac, Mexico (now part of Mexico City), there were several appearances to a peasant, Juan Diego. In the first appearance, Juan was on his way to Mass when he heard what sounded like birds. He went to investigate and found a woman who looked like a native princess. She said she was the Virgin Mary. Around her waist, she wore the familiar cultural sash that identified her as being pregnant. She asked for a church to be built on that site, which was formerly an Aztec temple (Aztecs were notorious for human sacrifice), so that she could hear petitions to heal the suffering of the Mexican people. Juan Diego went to the bishop, who of course was skeptical. The bishop asked for a sign to prove the lady's identity. Juan did not go directly back, as his uncle was ill. But when he did return and asked Mary for a sign, she instructed him to go to a place on the hill and gather roses. Juan was filled with disbelief because it was December and did not anticipate finding any flowers. However, he found the roses on the hill and gathered them in his cloak (*tilma*). Juan went back to the bishop and produced the flowers, which surprised the bishop because they were Castilian roses, not common in Mexico but instead indigenous to the bishop's homeland. But even more miraculous, the *tilma* had Mary's image exactly as in the vision Juan Diego had seen. The church was built, and the practice of human sacrifice of over 20,000 per year began to come to an end. Consequently, millions of natives were converted to Christianity. A final miracle of the *tilma* is that the cactus fibers only have a 20- to 30-year life at best. Yet the *tilma* remains completely intact and on display even today in Mexico City, with countless miracles attributed to it. There was no earthly way known at that time to have produced and preserved such an image without signs of deterioration.

Our Lady of Fatima

In Portugal from May 13 to October 13, 1917, the Virgin Mary appeared to three young children six times, and a seventh time to one of the girls (Lucia) alone. The message to the children was for the world, that peace would reign if her requests for prayer and fasting were listened to and obeyed. One of the messages stated that Russia was to be an instrument of chastisement to punish the world with a great evil that would come from there and spread globally. To avoid this, she asked for prayers for the conversion of Russia. The thought of Russia spreading evil was almost unimaginable, since Russia was known to be a Godly nation at that time. Suspecting the children were lying, the Portuguese officials threatened them. But as we know now from history, shortly after the apparitions, Russia was plagued with political upheaval that resulted in Atheism, Socialism, and Communism; it did indeed spread throughout the world. Ultimately, Mary has asked for daily praying of the Rosary for the intentions of peace and for the consecration of Russia. There was a spring of water at the site of the apparitions, and miracles from Fatima waters sent throughout the world occur even today.

55. Protestants object to the Rosary as worship of Mary. Do Catholics actually worship Mary?

To understand how Catholics view the Rosary, it is helpful to know its history. Although the prayers were a part of prayer life prior to formalizing the Rosary, its modern understanding came about during the 13th century and is associated with answering the heresies of a sect known as Albigensians. In his book, *Champions of the Rosary*, Fr. Donald Calloway of the Marians of the Immaculate Conception explains the history of how the Rosary came to us. Fr. Calloway states that the Albigensian sect taught that everything material was evil, and that a person's soul was trapped in an evil human body. Their teaching had a hugely heretical impact on the understanding of Christ as God and man, attacking the very core of the Catholic faith. At about that time, Spaniard Dominic Gusman (founder of the Dominican Order) spoke out against the Albigensians. Then in AD 1208, he engaged in a three-day silent retreat to pray and fast. On the third day, St. Dominic experienced a miraculous encounter with the Virgin Mary, who informed him that his preaching would receive power through the *Ave Maria* (Hail Mary). She said to "preach my Psalter." According to Fr. Calloway, the Marian Psalter was already in existence, however St. Dominic began a new way to pray it. His new method, under the instruction of Mary, was to divide the 150 Hail Marys into decades of 10 each. Each of those decades includes a mystery of Christ's life for specific meditation. As Fr. Calloway points out, these mysteries were a direct answer to the errors being promoted by the Albigensians. They centered on Christ's incarnation, passion, and resurrection. The name Rosary came later to depict the roses a young Franciscan brought to images of the Blessed Mother (Calloway, 2016, pp. 35-40).

One thing to note is that the Rosary never shows any deification of the Virgin Mary, but instead has always remained a devotion to God on the mysteries of the life, death, and resurrection of Christ. However, many people believe the repetition of the Hail Mary to be worship of her and nothing to do with God. This is far from the truth. The Rosary starts with the Nicene Creed, which is a summary of the tenets of the Christian faith. Each decade begins with the Our Father. Next, the Hail Mary begins with the annunciation from the angel to Mary in Luke, and then "Blessed art thou among women, and blessed is the fruit of thy womb" from Mary's cousin, Elizabeth. At the end of the prayer is, "Holy Mary, Mother of God, pray for us sinners now and at the hour of our death." (See Section VI for more on praying for intercession of the saints.) The Glory Be prayer is a Trinitarian affirmation prayer. To complete the Rosary is the Hail Holy Queen, or Salve Regina prayer. This prayer gives Mary honor (*hyperdulea*), yet shows a longing for her to show to us the "blessed fruit of thy womb, Jesus." As in all Mariology, Mary always brings us to her Son; she does not require or receive worship.

One might wonder what the real benefit of the Rosary might be to a Christian. According to Fr. Donald Calloway, "We live in a fallen world where fallen angels (demons) seek to destroy us. Such evil can only be overcome by having a greater weapon than the enemy possesses" (Calloway, 2016, p. 331). What greater prayer is a meditation on the life, death, and resurrection of Jesus Christ? Although the Hail Mary bears her name, that prayer and the entire Rosary is a meditative devotion on her Son, Jesus.

IX

The Eucharist

he Eucharist is one of the seven sacraments in the Catholic Church. However, most denominations do not view communion as a sacrament. Where Catholics believe Christ is present in body, blood, soul, and divinity in the Eucharist, most Protestants view it as symbolic. This section will explain Catholic doctrine on the Eucharist.

56. Does Scripture teach us that Communion is just bread and wine, as in Protestant tradition?

Whether or not one believes in literal transubstantiation is significant to faith in Christ, for the way we receive Communion says much about what we believe about Jesus. In passages about the Last Supper (Matthew 26:17-30, Mark 14:12-25, and Luke 22:7-20), Jesus says to take and eat, for it is his body and blood. Interpretation of the word "is" has been debated, and some say it is figurative. However, if we go to John 6:48-69 (the Bread of Life discourse), it becomes clear. The Jews who heard him instructing them to eat his flesh and drink his blood became agitated and angered. What appeared to them as cannibalism was explicitly forbidden in Jewish Law. They knew exactly what he was saying and that he meant it literally, so those disciples abandoned him. Yet it is Jesus' reaction to their departure that tells the full story in how to discern this passage. Jesus asked the remaining disciples if they also will leave, discovering who would remain faithful in the face of a difficult teaching. Then Simon Peter replied, "Master, to whom shall we go? You have the words of eternal life." Even further as their spokesman, St. Peter states in verse 69, "We have come to believe and are convinced that you are the Holy One of God." If Jesus had meant his words figuratively, he would have done what he always did when teaching his disciples: he would have explained it as a "parable." But instead, he continued on to his next point with them, referring to the "devil" who would betray him. Jesus is Truth, and for him to allow faulty teaching on this important issue is impossible. The Holy Eucharist, consecrated in accordance with Jesus' teachings at the Last Supper, by ministerial priests ordained in the Apostolic Order, is the literal body, blood, soul, and divinity of Jesus under the appearance of bread and wine. As the disciples who abandoned Jesus acknowledged, this is a very hard teaching. In fact, it is likely the most difficult of all the teachings in Christianity. Even today, the mystery of Eucharistic transubstantiation is still a mystery. Therefore, it is only through faith and believing Christ at his word that we can accept it.

57. Should Protestants believe early Church teachings about the Real Presence of Christ in the Eucharist?

From the earliest times in the Church, the Church Fathers reiterated what was already known and believed: the Eucharist is the body, blood, soul, and divinity of Our Lord. It is logical to embrace what was known and taught from the beginning, rather than reduce it to mere symbolism. Here is what just a few of the earliest Church Fathers have to say.

> "They abstain from the Eucharist and from prayer, because they confess not the Eucharist to be the flesh of our Saviour Jesus Christ, which suffered for our sins, and which the Father, of His goodness, raised up again." (Ignatius of Antioch, Epistle to Smyrnaeans,

7,1, c. AD 110). (St. Ignatius was a student of St. John the Apostle.)

"For not as common bread and common drink do we receive these; but in like manner as Jesus Christ our Saviour, having been made flesh and blood for our salvation, so likewise have we been taught that the food which is blessed by the prayer of His word, and from which our blood and flesh by transmutation are nourished, is the flesh and blood of that Jesus who was made flesh." (Justin Martyr, First Apology, 66, c. AD 110-165).

"[T]he bread over which thanks have been given is the body of their Lord, and the cup His blood..." (Irenaeus, Against Heresies, IV:18,4, c. AD 200). (Most influenced by St. Polycarp, who had known the apostles.)

These are but a few historical proofs that the Church Fathers consistently held the view of transubstantiation.

58. Since in John 6 the Jews, the disciples, and the apostles took Jesus literally (and Jesus did not correct them), why would Protestants take him only symbolically?

Basically, this comes down to interpretation, exegesis, and hermeneutics. With the break from Catholicism, Protestants were on their own without Magisterial guidance or historic holy Tradition passed down from apostles to the early Church Fathers. For more than 1000 years, the truth of the Holy Eucharist was accepted and understood because of these safeguards of Church doctrine. Once there was a break, the denominations and their leaders began to rely upon their own new interpretation of previously accepted Catholic doctrines. That is why for some (as the Lutherans), there is a partial belief called consubstantiation. For others, there is the belief of communion as either memorial or symbolic. Consequently, what was always known and accepted as true became new, heretical doctrine. Considering the importance of this issue with regards to understanding Christ in his fullness, the validity of the various interpretations is not possible. There is only one truth, and Christ could have only meant one thing by his statement: it is his body and blood, not something reduced to a symbolic act. Since the ministerial priesthood and apostolic succession is not retained in other churches, transubstantiation is only valid when bread and wine are consecrated by priests in the churches within the rites of the Catholic Church (Latin, Byzantine, Antiochian, Chaldean, Armenian, Alexandrian), as well as Eastern Orthodox churches and other ancient Christian churches that have apostolic succession. Even so, Protestants and others can receive Christ spiritually in their communion encounters, although not in a sacramental Eucharistic manner. Since to know Christ in his fullness is to receive him in his fullness, there is great joy in uniting with him through the Holy Eucharist.

59. If the Eucharist is so critical to life in Christ, why don't Catholics allow non-Catholics to partake with them?

Until the Protestant Reformation, to be Christian was understood to mean to be Catholic. In order to be part of the Church, the believer agreed to all the tenets of the faith as represented in Catholicism. Of all the beliefs, the Eucharist is considered the source and summit of the Christian life (*Catechism of the Catholic Church*, 1324). Holy Communion in the Eucharist is a sacrament in the Catholic Church, as opposed to merely a memorial symbol as in Protestantism. This sacrament is only available to those who still believe in the tenets of our faith, particularly in the Council of Trent declaration that the Eucharist is the Real Presence of Christ through transubstantiation (*Catechism of the Catholic Church*, 1378). In order to be one with each other in Christ, this belief is paramount. But there is also a desire to protect those who may not receive in this worthy manner, as stated in a Catholic Answers tract on Communion (2004):

> Scripture is clear that partaking of the Eucharist is among the highest signs of Christian unity: "Because there is one bread, we who are many are one body, for we all partake of the one bread" (1 Cor. 10:17). For this reason, it is normally impossible for non-Catholic Christians to receive Holy Communion, for to do so would be to proclaim a unity to exist that, regrettably, does not.
>
> Another reason that many non-Catholics may not ordinarily receive Communion is for their own protection, since many reject the doctrine of the Real Presence of Christ in the Eucharist. Scripture warns that it is very dangerous for one not believing in the Real Presence to receive Communion: "For anyone who eats and drinks without discerning

the body eats and drinks judgment upon
himself. That is why many of you are weak
and ill, and some have died" (1 Cor. 11:29–
30).

As one can see, there are spiritual implications outlined in Holy Scripture for those receiving unworthily,
and the Church takes those very seriously. The Catholic Church does not intend to withhold the Eucharist
to offend people. Instead, the Church understands that
the Eucharist is to be consumed only by those who
agree with Jesus' words, as defined in the Council of
Trent teaching, that the Eucharist literally is his body
and blood, and that they are Catholics in a state of grace
without mortal sin. That is the definition of true Communion in the faith among the faithful: that all are in
agreement and our hearts are prepared to receive him.

60. Is there physical evidence to support that Communion actually is the body and blood of Jesus?

If you are not familiar with Eucharistic miracles,
they have occurred during the Consecration where the
bread and wine become actual flesh and blood. These
phenomena are well-documented through painstaking
investigation. The very first Eucharistic miracle happened in AD 700 in Lanciano, Italy, then known as Anxanum. In accounts of this miracle, the priest who was to
celebrate Mass was having doubts about the Real Presence of Christ in the Eucharist. As he spoke the words of
Consecration, "This is my Body, This is my Blood," he
witnessed a transformation of the elements into living
flesh and blood. The many witnesses were convinced
of a miracle. Consequently, the archbishop ordered an

investigation. Many investigations of this first Eucharistic miracle, the most recent in 1981, have taken place. All have resulted in the same conclusion: the flesh is human flesh, and the blood is human blood. With the advent of modern chemistry came more details into this miracle. The flesh is cardiac, the blood has proteins found in fresh, normal blood, and there are no artificial chemicals or preservatives in it. Yet this miracle remains in Lanciano for all to see. This was the first such miracle, but there have been countless since then. The Church continues to research many of them, and those findings are made public. One unique discovery is that for each of them, the same blood type—AB Positive, or the universal type—is present. Even more miraculous is that it is the same blood type found upon the Shroud of Turin and the Holy Face of Manoppello, which is a facial burial cloth that bears the image of Christ and is digitally identical to the Shroud (Nasuti, 2010). There are countless such miracles that are Vatican approved, all of which must go through rigorous testing. In 2006 alone, there were over 120 being translated from Italian to English through the Real Presence Association. Reducing Communion to merely a symbolic gesture is hard to defend, although in one sense Protestants are correct with regards to their communion celebrations because there is no ordained priest in the Apostolic Order to consecrate their communion meal (i.e., transubstantiation does not take place). However, in light of the many Eucharistic miracles reported and researched in Catholicism, it is difficult to claim the Holy Eucharist to be merely a symbol.

X

Other Sacraments

he previous section gives reasoning for the Holy Eucharist as a sacrament. Although all of the sacraments are worthy of discussion, what follows is a discussion on a few of the remaining sacraments in the Catholic Church.

61. Is there evidence in Holy Scripture that there are indeed seven sacraments?

Denominational churches differ on the issue of sacraments, although most agree on baptism. However, in the Catholic Church there are seven sacraments. According to Catholic teaching in the *Baltimore Catechism*, "A sacrament is an outward sign instituted by Christ to give grace" (no. 304). Each sacrament finds its root in Christ and is sanctified by Him.

Baptism: Mark 16:15-16

Confirmation: John 7: 38-39 & 16:7, Acts 2:1-4

Holy Eucharist: John 6:48-59, Matthew 26:26-28, Mark 14:22-24

Confession or Penance: Matthew 18:15-18, Acts 19:17

Marriage: Matthew 5:31-32, Matthew 19:3-9

Last Rites or Extreme Unction: Mark 6:12-13, James 5:14-15

Holy Orders*: Acts 6:5-6, Acts 20:28, 1 Timothy 3:1-13, 1 Timothy 4:4-14

*Note: Holy Orders is understood in the context of the unbroken line of apostolic succession.

Baptism

62. Do Protestants have a universal view of baptism's significance or meaning?

The Great Commission is proof that baptism is of significance, as this was Jesus' command before leaving the world. Another way we know the importance of baptism is that Jesus' baptism marked the beginning of his public ministry. However, there are many conflicting views surrounding baptism. Some churches believe it is symbolic, while others say it is a sacrament necessary for the remission of sin. Some churches allow for infants to be baptized, while others have age requirements, ranging from twelve to adulthood. Methodology also widely varies, including everything from sprinkling to dunking. With such an important issue, certainly there should be a universally accepted definition that unites all non-Catholics; however, there is not. Most outside of Catholicism point to baptism as a symbol, not a saving sacrament. Baptism as symbolism is not found in Holy Scripture. To the contrary, there are many scriptural texts that point to baptism being sacramental. It is evident in Matthew 28:19, the Great Commission, that Jesus made baptism his final teaching. Such an important final word from Christ indicates that this was not merely symbolic. When Christ was baptized, the Holy Spirit came down upon him not in a symbolic act of approval, but as a visible sign of the significance of baptism as a means of imparting God's grace. Mark 16:16 tells us, "Whoever believes and is *baptized* will be saved..." Then in Acts 2:38, St. Peter speaking at Pentecost says, "Repent and be baptized, every one of you, in the name of Jesus Christ for the forgiveness of your sins; and you will receive the gift of the Holy Spirit." Forgiveness of sin is not symbolism, but a concrete infusion of grace. Also, in John 3:5 Jesus said, "Amen, amen, I say to you, no one can enter the kingdom of God without being born of water and Spirit." Clearly throughout Scripture, baptism is shown to be significant and for the forgiveness of sin.

Since the early Church, Christians have understood that baptism was for the remission of sin, even to the point of excommunicating others who falsely taught otherwise. The early Church writers, some taught by the apostles and others who were only one or two generations from Christ and the apostles, continued that teaching by writing very clearly that the purpose of baptism was for the forgiveness of sin (Epistle of Barnabas, Hermas, Ignatius of Antioch, Second Clement, Justin Martyr, Theophilus of Antioch, Clement of Alexandria, Tertullian, Hippolytus, Cyprian of Carthage, Aphraahat the Persian Sage, Cyril of Jerusalem, Basil the Great, Council of Constantinople I, Ambrose of Milan, and Augustine). One of the first references to baptism as a saving sacrament outside of Sacred Scripture is in the First Apology of Justin Martyr, where he writes,

> [the Eucharist], of which no one is allowed to partake but the man who believes that the things which we teach are true, and who has been washed with the washing that is for the remission of sins, and unto regeneration, and who is so living as Christ has enjoined (Justin Martyr, AD 153-155, Ch. 66).

These tenets are solidified within the Nicene Creed, which is a summary of the faith of the Church: "*I confess one baptism for the forgiveness of sins.*" Furthermore, Martin Luther wrote,

> "[6]...Baptism is no human trifle, but is instituted by God himself, moreover, that it is solemnly and strictly commanded that we must be baptized or we cannot be saved, lest anyone regard it as a trifling matter, like putting on a new red coat. [7] For it is of the greatest importance that we esteem baptism [8] excellent, glorious, and exalted..." (McCain, 2007, Concordia Lutheran Confessions, Large Catechism, 4:6-8).

All things considered, baptism as instructed by Christ and taught by our Church Fathers remains a sacrament for the remission of sin and the beginning of the salvation process.

63. Does the Bible support infant baptism?

Before answering this, consider Jesus' demeanor and welcome of children into the covenant in Luke 18:15-17. If Christ was aware of the importance of early introduction to him, we also should consider the significance of baptism for children. There are many Bible verses that support infant baptism. In Acts 16:27-33, not only was the jailor baptized but also "the rest of his household." It is reasonable to assume that children and perhaps infants were part of his household and, therefore, baptized. Households typically included old, young, infants, slaves, etc....virtually all who lived under the same roof were included in these moments of baptism (see also Acts 16:15, Acts 16:33, 1 Cor 1:16). Additionally, Colossians 2:11-12 indicates that baptism is to replace the practice of circumcision (Genesis 7:12), the method of bringing a newborn and all in the household into covenant with God. All of this supports that the practice of baptism included infants.

The early Church Fathers and councils also had much to say about infant baptism. Although there appears to be freedom in the practice, and even Gregory of Nazianaum suggests putting off baptism until the age of three unless there is a danger of death, Tertullian in AD 220 states that there should be sponsors who could help in the spiritual training of the child. This could point to the origin of selecting godparents. Other Church Fathers who supported infant baptism were numerous. Irenaeus wrote, "He [Jesus] came to save all through himself; all, I say, who through him are reborn in God: infants, and children, and youths, and old men..." (*Against Heresies* 2:22:4 [AD 189]). Hippolytus states, "Baptize first the children, and if they can speak for themselves let them do so. Otherwise let their parents or other relatives speak for them" (*The Apostolic Tradition* 21:16 [AD 215]). In Origen's writings, we find, "Every soul that is born into flesh is soiled by the filth of wickedness and sin...in the Church, baptism is given for the remission of sins, and, according to the usage of the Church, baptism is given even to infants. If there were nothing in infants which required the remission of sins and nothing in them pertinent to forgiveness, the grace of baptism would seem superfluous" (*Homilies on Leviticus* 8:3 [AD 248]). Further writings from the earliest Church Fathers include Cyprian of Carthage (*Letters* 64:2 and 64:5

[AD 253]), Gregory of Nazianz (*Oration on Holy Baptism* 40:7 and 40:28 [AD 388]), John Chrysostom (*Baptismal Catecheses in Augustine, Against Julian* 1:6:21 [AD 388]), and Augustine (*On Baptism, Against the Donatists* 4:24:31 [AD 400]; *The Literal Interpretation of Genesis* 10:23:39 [AD 408]; *Letters* 166:8:23 [AD 412]; and *Just Deserts of Sin, and the Baptism of Infants* 1:9:10, 1:24:34, 2:27:43 [AD 412]). In addition to this were two early Church council teachings at the Council of Carthage V (Canon 7 [AD 401]) and the Council of Mileum II (Canon 3 [AD 416]). The issue of infant baptism has deep roots in the Church and writings of the Church Fathers.

64. What is the proper method for baptism?

Baptism comes from the Greek word *baptizo*. Although it does mean to dip (as in 2 Kings 5:14), this is not its only meaning. In Luke 11:38, *baptizo* is used in describing washing before dinner. Obviously, that was not immersion. It means a cleansing. Another reference to baptism is in Acts 1. Jesus said the disciples would be baptized with the Holy Spirit. This was fulfilled at Pentecost, when the Holy Spirit poured down upon them. The *Didache* explains that baptism is to be done with "living" water, stating that water may instead be poured over the head three times while using the Trinitarian Form: Father, Son, and Holy Spirit (Laux, 1990, Ch. II). The only real requirements for baptism are the use of water and the Trinitarian Form.

Confession or Reconciliation

65. Protestants reject confessing sins to a priest, but is confession supported biblically?

We know from 1 John 1:9 that Christ promises to cleanse us of sin if we confess. But what way did he provide for that confession? Jesus gave that power to the first disciples and their successors when he said, "Receive the Holy Spirit. Whose sins you shall forgive they are forgiven them. Whose sins you shall retain they are retained" (John 20:23). When Christ gave them the Holy Spirit, it was a commission to forgive in his place when he was gone. That commission is continued on in the unbroken line of apostolic succession. In the earliest church, public confession was the norm. Even so, we read as early as AD 70 in the *Didache* (early writing known as *The Teaching of the Twelve Apostles*), and from subsequent early Church Fathers' writings that the Sacrament of Confession administered by a priest was practiced from the very beginnings of the Church.

Marriage

66. Since most Protestant churches permit divorce, is divorce actually allowed in the Bible?

In Matthew 5:32 and Matthew 5:19, Jesus instructs that divorce is only allowed in certain cases. The difficulty is in translation. The original Greek translation of the word in question is *porneia*, which is an illicit or unnatural relation. This would include close relations, incest, or homosexuality. In this Scripture, Jesus uses the word *porneia*, as such marriages are unnatural and invalid. However, the confusion arises when the word is translated as "adultery" or "unfaithfulness." Some translations use the word "adultery" due to another Scripture where Jesus spoke of someone committing adultery, looking at another's wife (Matthew 5:28). However, in this verse Jesus uses the word *mocheia*, the Greek word for adultery. Therefore, even though adultery is a grave sin, it is not a biblical reason for divorce; it is not the same word used in Matthew 5:32 (Trigilio, 2007). The correct translated word of *porneia*, with its inherent meaning, is why the Catholic Church does not view this passage to mean adultery as an "escape clause" from marriage. Instead, the Church defines any valid marriage as indissoluble.

67. In light of the fact that divorce is not permitted per Holy Scripture, how is it that divorce and remarriage is readily accepted in many Protestant churches?

Claiming Matthew 5:32, a number of denominations treat divorce as a distinct possibility. However, as seen in Question 66, if the Matthew 5:32 verse is not translated properly and the word in question is translated incorrectly as "adultery," it is easy to see how Protestant denominations might believe divorce and remarriage to be acceptable in cases of adultery. Consequently, when a person is divorced and remarried, they are still welcome in full participation in the majority of Protestantism — including participation in communion. Unfortunately, invalid divorce and the sin involved are many times overlooked by the congregation. There are even countless cases of ministers who have affairs, yet are able to remain in their ministry or leave for a time and return later. The sanctity of what God means to "join together" and "let no man put asunder" is effectively destroyed. Conversely, in Catholicism there is a very narrow allowance for annulment and remarriage, allowed for only if the marriage is found to have a defect at the time of the vows, making it then invalid. The subject of divorce points to how critical it is to use correct translations of Holy Scripture, as well as apostolic teachings from the early Church.

Holy Orders or the Priesthood

68. Does the Bible give support for people to use the title "Father" for priests?

Those who believe it is wrong to call a priest "Father" base it upon the words of Christ in Matthew 23:9, "Call no man your father on earth, for you have one Father who is in heaven." Unfortunately, those who use this verse as proof apply it in a way that is both illogical and does not reflect Christ himself or biblical foundations. First, if one truly believes that Christ's intent was to ban the word "father" except in reference to God the Father, it would violate the Fourth Commandment: Honor thy father and thy mother. We should all be in agreement that if Jesus was sinless, he would by definition have been true to his faith as a Jew. Jewish Law in the form of the Commandments was the basis for relationship to both God and man. Religious and social constructs were dependent upon this order, and family life was at the center of Jewish life. If we were to take Jesus to mean that children and adults should now completely disrespect their earthly fathers by refusing to address them as such, we would then imply that Jesus was encouraging sin. Second, the disciples themselves used the term "father" in combination with Abraham, when Stephen the First Martyr refers to "our father Abraham" (Acts 7:2). Then in Romans 9:10, Paul uses the term "our father Isaac." Clearly if the apostles understood Jesus to mean a ban on the word in these contexts, these passages would show defiance toward Christ's teachings. The more likely meaning is that Jesus was using an exaggeration in order to make a point. An explanation from Catholic Answers tract "Call No Man Father" (2004), says,

> Christ used hyperbole often, for example when he declared, "If your right eye causes you to sin, pluck it out and throw it away; it is better that you lose one of your members than that your whole body be thrown into hell" (Matt. 5:29, cf. 18:9; Mark 9:47). Christ certainly did not intend this to be applied literally, for otherwise all Christians would be blind amputees! (cf. 1 John 1:8; 1 Tim. 1:15). We are all subject to "the lust of the flesh and the lust of the eyes and the pride of life" (1 John 2:16).

> Since Jesus is demonstrably using hyperbole when he says not to call anyone our father — else we would not be able to refer to our earthly fathers as such — we must read his words carefully and with sensitivity to the

presence of hyperbole if we wish to understand what he is saying.

Further, there is evidence that the Bible plainly indicates the teaching in context had to do with Rabbinical practices emerging. Fr. Ray Ryland explains:

> Look again at the passage in which Jesus says we must call no one "father." In contrast to the attitudes of the Pharisees and others, Jesus is specifying the qualities Christian leaders must exhibit (Mt 23:1-12). The Pharisees aspired to being called "rabbi" (or "master" or "teacher"), leaders of schools of thought. Among the schools headed by teachers called "rabbi" there were divergences of belief, some of them in actual contradiction. A similar situation prevailed with regard to the term "father" (in Aramaic, *abba*, a title of honor). The title was given to well-known Jewish religious authorities of the past. As with "rabbi," so with "father." The term designated the progenitor of a particular, even contradictory, interpretation of the Jewish faith.
>
> Why did Jesus declare that no Christian leader is to be called "rabbi" or "father"? He was telling us that no leader may set up his own interpretation of the Catholic faith and seek followers for his opinions. The role of leaders in Christ's Church is faithfully to hand on Christ's teaching received through the apostles (Mt 28:19). The words of the apostle Paul epitomize the essential attitude

of the Christian teacher: "This is what I received from the Lord and in turn passed on to you" (1 Cor 11:23). Paul condemns in the church at Corinth "these slogans you have, like 'I am for Paul,' 'I am for Apollos,' 'I am for Cephas'" (1 Cor 1:12) (Ryland, n.d.).

As so often happens, when one verse is taken out of context and not considered with the passage as a whole, which includes historical context and biblical teaching, confusion and misinterpretations arise.

69. Do Protestant pastors have authority that can be traced back to St. Peter?

We first see the beginnings of how Christ would safeguard his Church by the establishment of priestly duties in an apostolic line in Luke 10:16. This verse 16 shows the significance of authority given the apostles to speak in Christ's place. Jesus says, "Whoever listens to you listens to me. Whoever rejects you rejects me. And whoever rejects me rejects the one who sent me." The first bishops are distinct representatives of Jesus, speaking with his same authority. Then in John 20:21-22 the resurrected Jesus, breathing the Holy Spirit upon them, sends the apostles out with the same power he was given by the Father. He authorizes them to forgive sins as part of this new authority. This priestly duty was specific to the new apostolic line he was establishing. Then binding and loosing was given in Matthew 18:18, also demonstrating the authority of priests in the apostolic line. Selection of those who would continue that line for future generations then became a critical endeavor. We see evidence of the seriousness of the task in Acts 1 with the replacement of Judas. It was very important that the replacement was one who was theologically sound and with them from the beginning. The method of selection relied upon God rather than a democracy.

However, when Jesus commissioned St. Peter as the visible head of the Church on earth in Matthew 16:18, he began a hierarchy which recognized the Bishop of Rome as pre-eminent. It is generally undisputed that St. Peter lived and died in Rome, where he was martyred (Wilhelm, J., 1907). From the time of St. Peter, the line from the Catholic Church has been completely uninterrupted with 266 popes from St. Peter to Pope Francis. In the early Church, apostolic succession was the test for whether or not teachings and doctrine were of Christ. In 2 Timothy 2:2 we find four generations of apostolic succession from St. Paul, to Timothy, to those Timothy teaches, and then to those they teach. The early Church Fathers became part of the unbroken line of succession, along with popes and bishops who then taught and ordained priests, as instructed in Titus 1:5 by St. Paul. "For this reason I left you in Crete so that you might set right what remains to be done and appoint presbyters in every town, as I directed you." Because of Luther's exit from the Church, he broke the line of succession for him and all subsequent denominations and organizations. Apostolic succession is the way teachings of the Catholic Church have remained pure since Christ.

XI

Questions About Martin Luther

ere is a brief look into the background and doctrines of Martin Luther as the father of the Protestant Reformation. (Note: For further information on one of Luther's primary complaints, indulgences, see Section XIII.)

70. Did Martin Luther's childhood influence his rebellion against the authority of the Catholic Church?

There are numerous sources that site the tumultuous household of Martin Luther as his reason for entering the monastery. According to an article in *New Advent Encyclopedia*, his father once beat him so mercilessly that he ran away from home and was so "embittered against him, that he had to win me to himself again" (Ganss, 1910). His mother, "on account of an insignificant nut, beat me till the blood flowed, and it was this harshness and severity of the life I led with them that forced me subsequently to run away to a monastery and become a monk" (Ganss). The same cruelty was the experience of his earliest school-days, when in one morning he was punished no less than fifteen times (Ganss). And from Catholic Online, regarding his reason to become an Augustinian Monk,

> Luther's sudden and unexpected entrance into the Augustinian monastery at Erfurt occurred July 17, 1505. The motives that prompted the step are various, conflicting, and the subject of considerable debate. He himself alleges, as above stated, that the brutality of his home and school life drove him into the monastery. Hausrath, his latest

biographer and one of the most scholarly Luther specialists, unreservedly inclines to this belief. The "house at Mansfeld rather repelled than attracted him" (Catholic Online, *Catholic Encyclopedia*, n.d.).

Furthermore, to "the question 'Why did Luther go into the monastery?' the reply that Luther himself gives is the most satisfactory." He himself again, in a letter to his father, in explanation of his defection from the old Church, writes, "when I was terror-stricken and overwhelmed by the fear of impending death, I made an involuntary and forced vow" (Catholic Online, *Catholic Encyclopedia*).

It is unfortunate that Luther's childhood in an abusive home may have been instrumental in creating mistrust and perhaps a disdain for authority, creating an invalid reason for his vocation. Papal authority, a huge theme for Luther, was the ultimate authority figure against which he would rebel.

71. Were there actually 95 separate issues raised by Martin Luther in his 95 Theses?

There actually were not 95 separate issues against the Catholic Church; many of the points raised were redundant. On the issue of indulgences, at least 40 of Luther's complaints addressed this (21, 31, 32, 34, 36, 37, 39, 40, 41, 42, 43, 44, 45, 46, 47, 48, 49, 50, 51, 52, 53, 54, 55, 56, 57, 64, 66, 67, 69, 71, 72, 73, 74, 75, 76, 79, 81, 85, 89, and 91). Some of the points listed are not even a complaint, but are more of a prelude sentence of description. Others numbers are the rephrasing of similar issues. Yet most people believe there were 95 serious complaints against the Catholic Church. This is false. Another issue in Luther's 95 Theses was the doctrine of purgatory. Again, this was redundantly phrased 15 times in separate points. Therefore, there has been a perpetuation of the false idea that Luther had 95 doctrinal complaints against the Church, when in actuality many of his points were redundant.

72. Did Martin Luther's 95 Theses justify a split from the Catholic Church?

As in the previous question, it becomes clear that the 95 Theses centered around three main issues: indulgences, purgatory, and papal authority. In actuality, each of these can rightfully be said to center around the authority of the Church. Once we embrace that the Church is the pillar and foundation of truth as 1 Timothy 3:15 states, the authority of the Church in its capacity as pillar and foundation is clear, rendering its teachings as authoritative. It is important to note that the Church never promoted the sale of indulgences (to be addressed in the section on indulgences). However, in subsequent years, the Church accomplished what Martin Luther did not: a true Reformation. The issue was the abuse of indulgences by certain Catholic bishops. Consequently, the problem was addressed at the Council of Trent (AD 1545-1564) where there was a definitive decree issued on Church teaching, forever settling the abuse (Catholic Answers, n.d., "Does the Catholic Church still sell indulgences?"). True reformation always transpires from within in order to improve (see Question 73). Instead, Luther rejected both the teaching and the authority of the Church, causing an upheaval that tore the Church apart instead of reforming it. The Protestant Reformation has continued to sunder itself into more than 30,000 splinters since the time of Luther's rebellion. Considering that the bulk of Luther's complaints surrounded a practice that was not even authorized by the Church, a split was not justified.

73. Did Martin Luther begin a true reformation, or was it possibly a rebellion?

According to *Merriam-Webster's Collegiate Dictionary* (2003), *reformation* is the process of improving something or someone by removing or correcting faults, problems, etc., whereas *rebellion* is an open opposition toward a person or group in authority, and refusal to obey rules or accept normal standards of behavior, dress, etc. When one reforms, he works from within to accomplish needed change that, in theory, will benefit the organization. As the definition implies, to reform by removing or correcting a fault, one must remain within the constraints of the organization; one cannot effect change in an organization in which he is not a member. In contrast, one who rebels has as his goal to separate himself from the established organization in defiance. It is literally incorrect to call the Protestant movement lead by Martin Luther a reformation movement. To be true to the definition, Luther would have remained a monk and sought to improve the Church from within. Instead, Luther's actions eventually caused scandal within the Church, brought about heretical changes in doctrine that resulted in denominations (a word meaning to rename), and lead others to rebel and abandon the Church along with him.

To be fair to Luther, the posting of his 95 Theses was not an unusual method at the University of Wittenberg. The door was a sort of "blackboard" for voicing academic challenges in order to reach understanding. However, in addition Luther sent his Theses to the archbishop, as well as his councilors. It was at the councilors' discretion that proceedings against Luther began for the apparent heretical nature of his Theses. From there, the issue snowballed into a multi-level dispute, with many players on both sides. What did not help Luther was his refusal to appear in Rome for a papal hearing, all the while preparing an inflammatory sermon attacking judgments by the Holy See. These were not the actions of one who wished to "reform," but rather one in rebellion.

Ironically, true reformation did occur within the Catholic Church (see Section XIII). However, it is important to note that the Catholic Church has never approved the sale of indulgences. During the 16th century, there were many abuses in this area that were in complete opposition to official Church teachings. Subsequently, the Council of Trent (AD 1545-1564) gave clear teaching in order to eliminate those abuses. In the Decree on Indulgences (Sess. 25), the Council provided methods for each bishop to report corruption. This is the true definition of a reform. The Church recognized and reeled in those who were falsely teaching that indulgences could be purchased. Although it took many years to bring all abusers to justice, we must remember that as we look through 21st century lenses, it is incorrect to apply our available methods to this process. Given the lack of technology and rapid transportation and given that the

Catholic Church has always followed protocol to insure properly addressing issues, the Council of Trent began a process that eventually was able to define and correct false teachings, abuses, and corruption throughout the Church with regards to the illegitimate selling of indulgences.

XII

Purgatory

uther's stand on purgatory was complicated and shaded by his railing against papal authority and indulgences as they related to purgatory. The following questions address whether the Catholic understanding of purgatory has merit and if so, from where it originated.

74. What does the Bible say is a requirement for entering Heaven?

In Revelation 21:27, we read that nothing unclean will be able to enter Heaven. And in Matthew 5:48, we are told to be perfect just as our heavenly Father is perfect. To claim the perfection of God would be blasphemous, because we daily sin in thought, word, deed, and lack of action. The real distinction on this issue is how we understand sinfulness and how it affects a person's faith journey (see the section on faith alone). Once we come to grips with that answer, we begin to understand the true requirements for entering Heaven.

75. Is purgatory in the Bible?

If a person expects to find the word "purgatory" in the Bible, he will come up empty. But neither will he find the word "trinity." Some concepts that are defined in Christianity are evident, and then given terms, others are revealed through divine revelation. In Jewish tradition, there was a method of atonement for souls so they could attain Heaven. As previously discussed, the seven books of canonized Scripture removed by the Protestant reformers contain a wealth of teachings important in understanding the fullness of Truth. One of those books is 2 Maccabees. In 2 Maccabees 12:39-46, we find this Jewish understanding of cleansing after death and the practice of praying for the dead in their final purging. The Catholic Church calls this purgatory, and it was surely understood by Christ himself as an orthodox Jew who practiced his faith. Since he never rejected that teaching, we as Christians also should not reject it. For further clarification, refer to Hebrews 12:22-23 (spirits made perfect), 1 Corinthians 3:13-15 (refining as if in fire in the light of Day — which is a reference to the great day of Yahweh or day of judgment), Matthew 12:32 (the phrase "in the age to come" is telling in that it proves that final forgiveness — purging in purgatory — is available after death, unless we blaspheme the Holy Spirit). Even Hebrews 10:14 implies that though Christ's goal is our perfection, we are not immediately "holy," but are being made holy. The verb is in present progressive passive tense, or present continuous tense, passive voice, which indicates it is ongoing. In addition, the previous references indicate that final perfection will transpire after our death prior to entering Heaven. Finally, in 1 Peter 3:19, it reads, "In it he also went to preach to the spirits in prison." This cannot be Hell, because that would mean Christ was mocking their doom. Instead, it was a message of hope to those in purgatory awaiting Heaven.

76. What else does the Bible teach us about purgatory?

The Old Testament teaches that there is punishment for sin after it is forgiven. In 2 Samuel 12:13-18, we see that even when God forgives and restores someone, there is a form of consequence that must be applied. Some of our due punishment occurs in purgatory after our death. Even a minor area of sin at the time of our death renders us unprepared for the requirement of purity in Heaven in that we may have venial sin that was not confessed. This sin would require atonement for the temporal punishment that was due in our earthly life. Hence, the need and purpose for purgatory. One thing to consider in understanding the need for purgatory is the full expectation of God for us as Christians. In James 2:9-13, it becomes clear that unless we can fully be perfect in our human form (i.e., commit NO transgression), we in effect are guilty of all of the law of God. That is a huge order, especially considering that we may not always be aware of where we have fallen short. Purgatory cleanses us to completion so that our souls can enter Heaven in perfection.

XIII

Indulgences

artin Luther's attack on indulgences stemmed from his great disdain of papal authority. The issue of indulgences is worthy of its own separate section here.

77. A great portion of Martin Luther's 95 Theses was an indictment against indulgences. What exactly is an indulgence?

According to the *Catechism of the Catholic Church,*

> An indulgence is a remission before God of the temporal punishment due to sins whose guilt has already been forgiven, which the faithful Christian who is duly disposed gains under certain prescribed conditions through the actions of the Church which, as the minister of redemption, dispenses and applies with authority the treasury of the satisfactions of Christ and the saints (CCC, 1471).

In sections 1472-1473 of the Catechism, we see that sin has a double consequence: eternal and temporal punishment. Although eternal punishment can be forgiven by seeking the Sacrament of Reconciliation, temporal punishment remains because of an unhealthy attachment to sin and, therefore, we are in need of purification. Purification transpires in purgatory; however, various charitable acts are a way to mitigate final punishment. By performing certain good works of mercy, along with prayer and penance with a contrite and loving heart, we can be brought back into favor with God. This mitigating process is what the Church calls indulgences.

78. Martin Luther's main issue was against the selling of indulgences, but was the selling of indulgences ever authorized by the Catholic Church?

While there was an apparent need for the Church to formally define the practice of indulgences, we should recognize that Luther's main accusation on the selling of indulgences was a misnomer:

> One never could "buy" indulgences. The financial scandal surrounding indulgences, the scandal that gave Martin Luther an excuse for his heterodoxy, involved alms— indulgences in which the giving of alms to some charitable fund or foundation was used as the occasion to grant the indulgence. There was no outright selling of indulgences. The *Catholic Encyclopedia* states: "[I]t is easy to see how abuses crept in. Among the good works which might be encouraged by being made the condition of an indulgence, almsgiving would naturally hold a conspicuous place.... It is well to observe that in these purposes there is nothing essentially evil. To give money to God or to the poor is a praiseworthy act, and, when it is done from right motives, it will surely not go un-rewarded" (Catholic Answers, 2004, Myths About Indulgences).

As with many doctrines, they at times need full defining at councils. In the 1500s, around the time St. Peter's Basilica was being rebuilt, there were abuses not corrected by priests and bishops in Germany. Because of these abuses, the Council of Trent addressed them in strong guidelines in order to eliminate them:

> Whereas the power of conferring Indulgences was granted by Christ to the Church; and she has, even in the most ancient times, used the said power, delivered unto her of God; the sacred holy Synod teaches, and enjoins, that the use of Indulgences, for the Christian people most salutary, and approved of [Page 278] by the authority of sacred Councils, is to be retained in the Church; and It condemns with anathema those who either assert, that they are useless; or who deny that there is in the Church the power of granting them. In granting them, however, It desires that, in accordance with the ancient and approved custom in the Church, moderation be observed; lest, by excessive facility, ecclesiastical discipline be enervated. And being desirous that the abuses which have crept therein, and by occasion of which this honourable name of Indulgences is blasphemed by heretics, be amended and corrected, It ordains generally by this decree, that all evil gains for the obtaining thereof, — whence a most prolific cause of abuses amongst the Christian people has been derived, — be wholly abolished. But as regards the other abuses which have proceeded from superstition, ignorance, irreverence, or from what soever other source, since, by reason of the manifold corruptions in the places and provinces

where the said abuses are committed, they cannot conveniently be specially prohibited; It commands all bishops, diligently to collect, each in his own church, all abuses of this nature, and to report them in the first provincial Synod; that, after having been reviewed by the opinions of the other bishops also, they may forthwith be referred to the Sovereign Roman Pontiff, by whose authority and prudence that which may be expedient for the universal Church will be ordained; that this the gift of holy Indulgences may be dispensed to all the faithful, piously, holily, and incorruptly (Waterworth, J., ed., 1848).

The Church recognized the scandal created by selling indulgences and acted within the scope of the Church to address it formally, forever defining it as illicit. However, keep in mind that it was considered illicit before the Council of Trent decree. The Church never has condoned or allowed the sale of indulgences.

79. Protestants claim that Pope Julius II sold indulgences for the rebuilding of St. Peter's Basilica. Is that true?

If we understand the Church teaching on indulgences, we know that it would never have been an authorized practice. The indulgence offered was technically not something for sale. Instead, it was received as a donation to the effort, similar to how Protestants might view the grace of God extended to one who feeds the poor or contributes to a building fund. Also, we must remember that an indulgence is never a forgiveness of sin. The reception of donations for the rebuilding of St. Peter's Basilica was completely in line with the teaching that joyful almsgiving for God's purposes are always voluntary donations and never attached as a purchase price for favor. One interesting note is that indulgences are offered also for sacrifices of prayer; this was likely also available during the rebuilding of St. Peter's Basilica.

80. Do Protestants engage in anything similar to indulgences?

It depends upon how one defines an indulgence. Those outside the Church engage in good works, donate to building funds, pray, and evangelize. Although not formally defined in most cases, there is an inherent desire and hope of God's favor as a reward for such activity. It is an unspoken, yet hoped for, result of doing the good work of God while on earth. Though no one (Catholic nor Protestant) believes he is "buying" his way into Heaven, each person knows the goodness of God and the favor he extends toward those doing his will and work. According to Catholic teaching, it is always considered a good thing to help the poor. However, our motives should be right. Catholics are not intending to "purchase" their way to Heaven. Instead, our final punishment is somewhat mitigated in the good works we do, as we align our behavior and hearts more toward Christ. Practically speaking, the only difference between Catholics and Protestants is terminology. Protestants will say they are doing good in the Name of Christ in thanksgiving to God. The Catholic Church agrees, and formally recognizes its benefits and gives the practice a name: indulgences.

XIV

Church Fathers

T he relevance in studying the history of the Catholic Church by knowing the Church Fathers is best stated by Blessed John Henry Newman, Anglican convert to the faith: "To be deep in history is to cease to be Protestant."

81. Is there value for Protestants to study the early Church Fathers?

When a person desires to know about the past, he can best obtain truthful information either from people who lived at that time, or those they taught. Such is the case with Catholic Church teachings and the early Church Fathers. The best way we readily understand the Church as it was passed down from the apostles is by studying the Church Fathers and their writings. There we find worship in the form of the Mass, and deep beliefs that continue to be part of the Catholic Church. Here are some examples with regards to important issues.

- Justin Martyr's writings (AD 150-160) include the elements of the Catholic Mass, which are still practiced today.
- Ignatius of Antioch in his Letter to the Romans 7:3 (AD 110) and his Letter to the Smyrnaeans 6:2-7:1 (AD 110) states that the Eucharist is the flesh and blood of the Savior, which is just as Jesus taught in the Bread of Life discourse of John 6. Other Fathers of the Church who believed in the Real Presence of Christ in the Eucharist were Irenaeus, Justin Martyr, Clement of Alexandria, Tertullian, Origen, and others. They all included this truth in their various writings.

- Jerome, along with St. Ignatius, Polycarp, Irenaeus, Justin Martyr, and Augustine (along with others) all professed the understanding of Mary's perpetual virginity, as it was taught and passed down in holy Tradition by those who knew her and her family. There was also a relevant historical document around AD 120 called the Protoevangelium of James, which addresses this, less than 60 years after Mary's earthly life ended. Although this document is not elevated to the level of Holy Scripture, it also is not in the category of Gnostic heretical writings. Instead, as it reflects many traditions known by the early Church, it is thus considered useful.

These are only a few teachings that came from the apostles and were passed down to the early Church and written by the Fathers of the Church. The significance is the unbroken apostolic line from which these teachings come. The apostle John taught Polycarp as his disciple. In turn, Polycarp became a teacher of apostolic truth and Tradition. He then taught Irenaeus, one of the greatest Christian apologists and theologians. Apostolic Tradition and writings of the early Church are ways of knowing the fullness of the Christian Faith.

82. When Church Fathers wrote about "the church," was it the Catholic Church?

There are some who state that the term catholic means "universal." In one sense, that is correct. From its Greek roots, we know it means "according to the whole." As early as the late first and into the second centuries, the term Catholic was used to indicate the true and universal Church, as opposed to heretical sects. Fairly quickly the Church understood the term as a means of separating themselves from heresies. Consequently, the creeds were written in order to promote the Catholic faith as the one true faith. Church Fathers began to use the term for the Church as early as AD 110. According to a Catholic Answers tract on what the word "Catholic" means (2004), there is an abundance we can discover by reading the early Church Fathers. Ignatius of Antioch, in his Letter to the Smyrneans 8:2, states that "...just as wherever Jesus Christ is, there is the Catholic Church." Ignatius called the Roman Church "...worthy of God, worthy of honor, worthy of the highest happiness" and the church that "resides over love, is named from Christ, and from the Father." In the "Martyrdom of Polycarp" 16:2 (AD 155), we read that Polycarp was the bishop of the Catholic Church in Smyrna. In the Muratorian Canon Fragment (AD 177) there is reference to the letters of Paul being "...regarded as holy in the Catholic Church, in ordering churchly discipline." Turtullian in "Demurrer Against the Heretics" (AD 200) states that certain men who lived in the not so distant past were "...believers in the doctrine of the Catholic Church, in the church of Rome under the episcopate of the blessed Eleutherius..." (13th pope). In other words, since the earliest times, the Church Christ founded has been called the Catholic Church, and it remains so today. Throughout Church history, we find evidence from the writings of Church Fathers, bishops, and several councils (I Nicaea, I Constantinople, Chalcedon), as well as in the Apostles' Creed and the Nicene Creed that recognizes the only non-schismatic church that remains unbroken since the time of Jesus Christ: the Catholic Church.

XV

Social Issues

arious denominations each have their own view on same-sex attraction and relationships, though we have seen those views change over time. Some religious organizations allow for homosexual pastors and perform same-sex marriages. Those outside the Catholic Church also differ on the indissolubility of marriage, contraception, and abortion. In the next several questions, we will explore what God has to say in his Word about some of the issues, along with some teachings from the Church Fathers.

83. Where in the Old Testament can we find definitive teaching against same-sex attraction?

To begin, we see in Genesis 19, where two angels in disguise visit Sodom. They go to see Lot, who shelters them. In the night, men of Sodom come to Lot demanding the male guests be given to them for their pleasure. Lot refuses, and even offers his virgin daughters to them, although the homosexual men refuse that offer. It is ironic how this story in recent times of homosexual activism has been morphed into a story of a lack of hospitality. However, until recently scholars were clear that Sodom was destroyed for the sin of homosexuality. In Ezekiel 16:50, the Bible speaks of Sodom committing abominable things, likely sexual sin.

However, the story of Sodom and Gomorrah is not the only Old Testament reference to the sin of homosexuality. In Leviticus 18:22 and 20:13, there are specific references to it being an abomination for a man to "lie down" with a man, or a woman with a woman. In fact, the punishment was death. In light of these passages, it is clear that the Old Testament condemns homosexual relations.

Same-sex Relations

84. Were the teachings in the New Testament consistent with the Old Testament, or did the New Covenant change the view of same-sex sin?

In Romans 1:26-28 and 32, there is a teaching by St. Paul. He states in the preface to this passage that when people begin to worship things other than God, they will exchange the Truth for a lie. The passage outlines these "lies" as women giving up natural, heterosexual relations for the unnatural (same-sex), and men as well, lusting for men instead of seeking the natural relationships God provided for them in women. Then in 1 Corinthians 6, St. Paul warns all again that homosexual behavior will keep them from inheriting the kingdom of God. We also are reminded of the Sodom and Gomorrah story in Jude 1:7, where Sodom and Gomorrah are described in this way: "...indulged in sexual promiscuity and practiced unnatural vice, serve as an example by undergoing a punishment of eternal fire."

But what if a person only wants to rely on Christ's teachings? Jesus referred to the sin of Sodom and Gomorrah in Matthew 10:15. The passage is describing the apostles going out to bring God's Truth to people in a town. If the people reject the Truth, Jesus says that it would be "...more tolerable for the land of Sodom and Gomorrah on the day of judgment than for that town."

His reference to Sodom and Gomorrah in this comparison shows the seriousness of the sins in those towns. Consequently, the Old Testament and the New Testament, including a teaching from Jesus, are completely consistent in condemning same-sex sin.

85. Since the Bible is very clear on homosexual relations, why is it that so-called gay marriage is approved in many Protestant churches?

As with many issues surrounding biblical understanding, the key is how a church defines authoritative teaching. Given the large number of Church Fathers who spoke against homosexuality (the *Didache*, Justin Martyr, Clement of Alexandria, Tertullian, Novatian, Cyprian of Carthage, Arnobius, Eusebius of Caesarea, Basil the Great, John Chrysostom, Augustine, and the *Apostolic Constitutions*), it is evident that those who were closest to Christ and the apostles' teachings understood it as sin. These teachings were passed down in the deposit of faith held within Catholic doctrine, and the Church maintains them. However, since the time of the Protestant Reformation, denominationalism lacks the benefit of apostolic tradition, as well as a mechanism of ultimate authority. Denominations and even individuals can each view biblical truths through their personal understanding of Scripture. And although it is true that the Word of God never changed on this issue, society and norms have. Many denominations decide on issues like a democracy, voted on by an elected board of deacons and elders, and elected boards will always reflect the values of society, as best they understand it. Hence, we find a multitude of interpretations within non-Catholic churches on this critical matter of sexual sin. The Catholic Church may have individual members who do not either understand or agree on this or other doctrinal issues, but the official teachings and doctrines have remained the same for 2000 years.

Contraception

86. Although Protestants generally approve of it, what are the biblical teachings on contraception?

In Genesis 38:8-10, Onan was put to death for the sin of contraception. Onan used a contraceptive method in order to avoid fulfilling his Jewish duty of fathering children for a dead brother. In Jewish Law, the punishment for avoiding this duty would have been public humiliation. We see this in Deuteronomy 25:7-10, where the law is described. So, why was Onan put to death? The only explanation is that his crime was more serious for the use of a contraceptive method. One could surmise that since God is the giver of life, to deny the possibility of life in the marital act is defying God and usurping God's role, which makes sense of the death of Onan in this case. There is no other reasonable explanation for Onan's punishment from God. The Catholic Church regards all contraception as interference with God's role as the giver of life. Therefore, all contraception is condemned.

87. Has the view of almost every Protestant denomination over the years changed regarding contraception?

Prior to the 1930s virtually all churches, both Protestant and Catholic, were against contraception. However, in 1930 there was a conference involving the Anglican church (1930 Lambeth Conference). As often happens, public opinion and pressure caused a shift so that there might be certain situations to allow for contraception. However, once they ventured on the slippery slope, they soon completely succumbed, opening the door for other denominations to follow suit. The original stand, true to the Bible, remains consistent in the Catholic Church that contraception is contrary to God's laws and is sinful.

88. Is there extra-biblical evidence that the current Protestant perspective on contraception is wrong?

One of the biggest reasons to view contraception in a negative light is the concept of natural law. Natural law makes statements on the things that relate to nature, and are a basis for human ethics and principles. Procreation falls easily into this understanding. The only real observable and quantitative outcome of sexual relations is procreation. To deliberately thwart that purpose is to oppose the natural law. However, in addition there is more recent evidence regarding common contraceptive methods. Several of the methods have been proven to be abortifacients, or methods which actually destroy a fertilized egg—the beginning of life. The "pill," IUDs, RU-486, morning after pills (Plan B), Norplant, Depo-Provera, Methotrexate, and Misoprostol are all abortifacients, causing the demise of a fertilized egg.

Since science defines and proves that human life begins at conception, and the survival of the species depends on life, it is against natural law to deliberately destroy life, including life in the womb.

89. Can the pill be said to end a human life, and if so, shouldn't it be considered wrong by both Catholics and Protestants?

The argument has been made that if one defines abortion as the ending of an established pregnancy after implantation, then the pill would not fall into this category because it prevents attachment in the uterus and is not implanted. However, if we want to define the ending of a human life as illicit, the pill fits the category according to medical science, particularly embryologic science. Embryologic science has defined that life begins at the moment of fertilization or conception. Human embryology and teratology (considered an undisputed authority in embryology) states,

> Although life is a continuous process, fertilization is a critical landmark because, under ordinary circumstances, a new, genetically distinct human organism is thereby formed.... The combination of 23 chromosomes present in each pro-nucleus results in 46 chromosomes in the zygote. Thus the diploid number is restored and the embryonic genome is formed. The embryo now exists as a genetic unity (O'Rahilly, Ronan and Muller, Fabiola, 1996, pp. 8, 29).

Therefore, most methods of contraception are the means of ending an innocent human life, which is always considered an intrinsic evil. Both Catholics and Protestants should consider use of the pill and other contraception wrong for this very reason. In the Catholic Church, contraception, which includes the pill, is considered morally unacceptable (CCC, 2399).

Abortion

90. Even though there is no firm Protestant doctrine against abortion, are there any biblical or early Church writings that oppose abortion?

Psalm 139 clearly shows that God knew us and knit us in our mother's womb. That would seem to indicate that to abort a child who has been conceived is to interfere with a process in which God is intimately involved. Tertullian, an early Christian writer, referred to Exodus 21:22-24 in condemning abortion. That Scripture states, "When men have a fight and hurt a pregnant woman, so that she suffers miscarriage, but no further injury, the guilty one shall be fined as much as the woman's husband demands of him...but if injury ensues, you shall give life for life..." This was explained by Tertullian as the "law of retribution" (*lex talionis*). It calls for justice for the innocent child who was murdered in the process. In *Didache* 2:1-2 [AD 70], we read that, "...you shall not use potions, you shall not procure [an] abortion." The *Didache* is considered the teaching of the twelve apostles, and thus carries great weight.

XVI

The Pope

he Bishop of Rome, or Pope, has historically been acknowledged as pre-eminent in Catholicism. This section will address his origin.

91. Since the time of Martin Luther, do Protestants have an ultimate authority to determine questions of faith and morals?

Protestants may state that the Bible along with the Holy Spirit is their ultimate authority. However, as we have seen, if interpretation of Holy Scripture is left to each denomination, pastor, Bible study leader, or individual, it is easy to come up with vastly different meanings of critical passages in Scripture. It seems that each denomination has their own method of defining the meaning of Scripture, but they vary greatly one from the other. Sometimes those definitions even change over time, depending upon the pastor in charge or even the governing boards. At times it is said that all the denominations agree on the "essentials"; however, there is no exhaustive list of those essentials, nor how the passages regarding those essentials should be interpreted. Conversely, Holy Scripture tells us that Jesus established a Church to lead us. Tim Staples states, "The historical record also tells us that Jesus Christ established a Church — not a book — to be the foundation of the Christian faith (Matt. 16:15-18; 18:15-18; cf. Eph. 2:20; 3:10, 20-21; 4:11-15; 1 Tim. 3:15; Heb. 13:7, 17)" (Staples, 2007). To have many "authorities," all of whom disagree in some critical areas, is not the sign of Christ's Church.

92. Did Jesus actually give St. Peter authority to be the visible head (Pope) of the Church?

Jesus gave authority to Peter and his successors when he said: "Truly I tell you, whatever you *bind on earth* will be bound in heaven, and whatever you loose on earth will be loosed in heaven" (Matthew 18:18). Interesting to note is that binding and loosing were terms familiar to rabbis. They meant to forbid and permit in reference to interpretation of the Law, and to condemn or acquit. It is evident that Jesus conferring this upon Peter and subsequent popes was for the purpose of authority in doctrine in order to lead the Church of the future, and for authority in discipline. In other words, it is the establishment of the powers of the papacy and bishops, with the Seat of Peter in preeminence (Armstrong, 1997, pp. 32-35). Also, refer to Question 9 for an understanding of Christ commissioning St. Peter as the rock.

93. Are there other scriptural and early Church proofs that St. Peter was recognized as the visible head of the Church?

We have already established that Christ established Peter as the rock, upon which the Church would be built. We can also look to the Scriptures to see the primacy of St. Peter. St. Peter is mentioned 191 times in the Gospels. The next in line is St. John, only at 48 times. There are at least 50 times the New Testament points to St. Peter's authority, given by Jesus. It is apparent that Christ was giving Peter the distinct role as visible head, or Pope, to lead the church on earth (Armstrong, 1997). In addition to Holy Scripture, the early Church Fathers wrote extensively on the primacy of St. Peter as head of the Church (Tertullian, Letter of Clement to James, the Clementine Homilies, Cyprian of Carthage, Firmilian, Ephraim the Syrian, Optatus, Ambrose of Milan, Pope Damusus I, Jerome, Augustine, Council of Ephesus, Sechnall of Ireland, Pope Leo I, Council of Chalcedon). One strong proof of Peter as visible head of the Church is Christ giving the keys of the kingdom to him. Dave Armstrong, Protestant convert, writes on the historical significance of the keys:

> The "power" of the keys has to do with ec-
> clesiastical discipline and administrative
> authority with regard to the requirements
> of the faith, as in Isaiah 22:22 (see Is 9:6;
> Jb 12:14; Rv 3:7). From this power flows the
> use of censures, excommunication, absolu-
> tion, baptismal discipline, the imposition of
> penances and legislative powers. In the Old
> Testament, a steward, or prime minister, is a
> man who is "over a house" (Gn 41:40; 43:19;
> 44:4; 1 Kgs 4:6; 16:9; 18:3; 2 Kgs 10:5; 15:5;
> 18:18; Is 22:15, 20-21) (Armstrong, 1997).

Here are some of the early church writings on the pre-eminence of the Bishop of Rome:

> "[T]he blessed Peter, the chosen, the preemi-
> nent, the first among the disciples, for whom
> alone with himself the Savior paid the tribute
> [Matt. 17:27], quickly grasped and under-
> stood their meaning. And what does he say?
> 'Behold, we have left all and have followed

you' [Matt. 19:27; Mark 10:28]" (*Who Is the Rich Man That Is Saved?* 21:3–5 [AD 200]).

~Clement of Alexandria

"[T]he Lord said to Peter, 'On this rock I will build my Church, I have given you the keys of the kingdom of heaven [and] whatever you shall have bound or loosed on earth will be bound or loosed in heaven' [Matt. 16:18–19]. . . . Upon *you*, he says, I will build my Church; and I will give to *you* the keys, not to the Church" (*Modesty* 21:9–10 [AD 220]).

~Tertullian

"[Christ] made answer: 'You are Peter, and upon this rock will I build my Church. . . .' Could he not, then, strengthen the faith of the man to whom, acting on his own authority, he gave the kingdom, whom he called the rock, thereby declaring him to be the foundation of the Church [Matt. 16:18]?" (*The Faith* 4:5 [AD 379]).

~Ambrose of Milan

"'But,' you [Jovinian] will say, 'it was on Peter that the Church was founded' [Matt. 16:18]. Well . . . one among the twelve is chosen to be their head in order to remove any occasion for division" (*Against Jovinian* 1:26 [AD 393]).

~Jerome

"Among these [apostles] Peter alone almost everywhere deserved to represent the whole Church. Because of that representation of the Church, which only he bore, he deserved to hear 'I will give to you the keys of the kingdom of heaven'" (*Sermons* 295:2 [AD 411]).

~Augustine

"Philip, presbyter and legate of [Pope Celestine I] said: 'We offer our thanks to the holy and venerable synod, that when the writings of our holy and blessed pope had been read to you . . . you joined yourselves to the holy head also by your holy acclamations. For your blessednesses is not ignorant that the head of the whole faith, the head of the apostles, is blessed Peter the apostle'" (*Acts of the Council*, session 2 [AD 431]).

~Council of Ephesus

94. Is it reasonable to believe that Christ would begin the Church, install Peter to lead it, and then after Peter's death leave the church without an earthly head or authority?

To answer this, we need to ask ourselves if the Church Christ left us was meant to be a democracy. Archbishop Fulton Sheen explains it well. He said there were three possible forms of government for the Church's mystical body: democratic, aristocratic, or theocratic. A democratic form leaves leadership dependent upon a majority rule, where everyone has a different opinion. This is mob rule. An aristocratic government is ruled by an elite or privileged upper class. It is an appeal to an aristocracy. This is tyrannical rule. It would have been in complete contrast to the teachings of Christ. However, in the theocratic form God chooses one man, as he did with Abraham, Isaac, Jacob, and Moses, then guides that man into holy leadership. We are shown that Christ made an appeal to the democratic form when he asked who the people said he was. However, he then asked who the apostles said he was. St. Peter, speaking for all, steps forward with the answer: the Christ, the Son of the Living God. This sets in motion the theocratic government intended for the Church, with one man preeminent and speaking for all on matters of faith and doctrine (Sheen, Archbishop Fulton, n.d.). Christ promised that the gates of Hell would not prevail against the Church, but if there is no visible authority to guide the Church it is open to chaos and heresy. That is not what Christ promised. Yet, since the Protestant Reformation, there have been multiple divisions, each claiming "authority" and being the true representation of Christianity. Apostolic succession of popes and bishops is the way Christ's Church has been safeguarded, beginning with St. Peter all the way through to Pope Francis. At this point, 266 successive bishops of Rome (popes) have occupied the Seat of Peter.

XVII

Conclusion

"What is truth?"
Pontius Pilate, at the Trial of Jesus Christ
(John 18:38)

95. What is truth, and does it matter?

If you were to query Catholics and Protestants on the importance of truth with respect to their religious beliefs on a scale of 1-10, it would likely be close to if not exactly at ten. For all those who claim Christ, it is because they have found truth in him. If you were to follow up that question with one that asked if each person believed their respective faith tradition to be true, again the responses would be resounding. However, is that possible? Considering the number of tenets of faith that are seemingly of paramount significance, yet whose doctrines are in complete contrast with others, there would be no way to justify accepting all as completely valid and true.

Marcus Grodi is a former Protestant minister who journeyed to Catholicism after more than 15 years in ministry. He is the founder and president of the Coming Home Network International, which serves those who are in the process of that same journey. Within his website are stories of many individuals, each of whom has discovered that the fullness of truth lies within the Catholic Church. Their discernment nearly always takes them to the historical foundations of the Church, where they find the one place where truth and authority lives. For many of these people, it is not as simple as going from the Presbyterian church to the Baptist church down the street. Quite the contrary, some have had to abandon pastoral ministries. Others have lost jobs or family and friends. But for all, the call from Christ to the Church he founded in AD 33 is too compelling to ignore.

In 2015, Don Johnson Evangelical Ministries released the movie titled, *Convinced*. Don is a convert to the faith. He began his adult faith journey as an evangelical, receiving university degrees at two Protestant universities. He then received his M.A. in Theology from Franciscan University in Steubenville, Ohio. His ministry is dedicated to proclaiming the gospel through media. To that end, his movie *Convinced* is a documentary that chronicles the lives of several converts, many of whom are well-known to Catholics. Although each has his or her own story, once they did their research into Catholicism they all came to conclusions expressed in one of the most moving segments near the end of the film (Johnson, 2015):

"Because Catholicism is true."
~Brandon Vogt, apologist and author

"It is true."
~Devin Rose, apologist and author

"It's true."
~Patrick Coffin, apologist, author, and radio host

"I found it to be true in the big and small things."
~Leah Libresco, author

"Because I truly believe that is where the truth is."
~David Currie, author

"What I concluded almost against my will was that Catholicism is true."
~Jason Stellman, former Presbyterian pastor

"All this is real. The truths of the faith, the things that the Church teaches are not just theories. They're statements about what the universe is really like."
~Mark Shea, apologist and author

"Aristotle said this in the 4th century BC: all men desire to learn the truth. So if you want to live by truth as opposed to falsehood, everybody at least should have the intellectual honesty to investigate the Catholic Church."
~Kenneth Howell, former Presbyterian pastor, professor, and author

"God loves us and wants us to be a part of his family. What I found in the Catholic Church is that family."
~Matthew Leonard, Director of the St. Paul Center for Biblical Theology

"It's the ark of salvation, it is an unruly place to be sure, it is a lot like the ark in many respects, it's not a clean and tidy and odor free environment, that's for sure, but it's the ark of salvation."
~Patrick Madrid, apologist and radio host

"It's the family of God that God established for our salvation."
~John Bergsma, professor, Franciscan University

"This is finding the pearl of great price, I mean to be Catholic is the most...It's really the most beautiful thing that you can do with your life."
~Taylor Marshall, former Anglican priest, apologist, and author

"Being received into the church and then receiving Communion was experientially different and it was if, especially the Eucharist, as if a veil was pulled away...as if I was...I was finally really touching, tasting, experiencing...By far the best thing I have ever done."
~Holly Ordway, professor, Houston Baptist University

"Sometimes people ask me if my life is better or worse now that I'm Catholic, and I never knew how to answer the question. Eventually I came to see that that's because it was the wrong question. It's not that my life is better or worse now that I'm Catholic. My life has started now that I'm Catholic."
~Jennifer Fulwiler, author and talk show host

These individuals and countless others, through honest research into the Catholic Church, have all come to the same conclusion: it is true. To reiterate what was stated in the Introduction, we do not expect that this book will instantly bring you to Catholicism. But we pray that we have provided enough evidence for you to desire to research for yourself whether or not the Catholic Church is the true Church that Christ founded. Why is this even important?

Because truth matters...and its consequences are eternal.

References List

Akin, James. (1996). "The Practical Problems of Sola Scriptura." Retrieved from http://www.ewtn.com/library/ANSWERS/PRACTICL.htm

Akin, James. "Salvation Past, Present, and Future." Retrieved from http://jimmyakin.com/salvation-past-present-and-future

Armstrong, Dave. (2012). *The Quotable Augustine: Distinctively Catholic Elements in His Theology.* Lulu Press.

Armstrong, Dave. (1997, January/February). "The Pre-Eminence of St. Peter: 50 New Testament Proofs." *Our Sunday Visitor.*

Barber, Michael. "The Lost Tomb of Jesus?" Retrieved from http://www.catholic.com/video/the-lost-tomb-of-jesus

Barth, Karl. (1961). *Church Dogmatics.* Louisville, KY: T&T Clark Ltd by Westminster John Knox Press.

Barrett, David B., Kurian, George T., and Johnson, Todd M. (2001). *World Christian Encyclopedia* (2nd ed.) (Vol. I). New York, NY: Oxford University Press.

Calloway, Fr. Donald, MIC. (2016). *Champions of the Rosary.* Stockbridge, MA: Marian Press.

Calloway, Fr. Donald, MIC. (2013). *Under the Mantle.* Stockbridge, MA: Marian Press.

Catechism of the Catholic Church. (1995). New York, NY: Doubleday.

Catholic Answers. (n.d.). "Does the Catholic Church still sell indulgences?" Retrieved from http://www.catholic.com/quickquestions/does-the-catholic-church-still-sell-indulgences

Catholic Answers. (2004). "Call No Man 'Father.'" Retrieved from http://www.catholic.com/tracts/call-no-man-father

Catholic Answers. (2004). "Immaculate Conception and Assumption, a Catholic Answers Tract." El Cajon, CA: Catholic Answers.

Catholic Answers. (2004). "Myths About Indulgences." Retrieved from http://www.catholic.com/tracts/myths-about-indulgences

Catholic Answers. (2004). "Relics." Retrieved from http://www.catholic.com//tracts/relics

Catholic Answers. (2004). "What 'Catholic' Means." Retrieved from http://www.catholic.com/tracts/what-catholic-means

Catholic Answers. (2004). "Who Can Receive Communion?" Retrieved from http://www.catholic.com/tracts/who-can-receive-communion

Currie, David B. (1996). *Born Fundamentalist, Born Again Catholic*. San Francisco, CA: Ignatius Press.

Epiphanius (of Salamis). (AD 376). *Medicine Chest Against All Heresies*.

Eusebius (of Cesarea). (AD 340). *Church History*.

Ganss, H. (1910). Martin Luther. In *The Catholic Encyclopedia*. New York: Robert Appleton Company. Retrieved from http://www.newadvent.org/cathen/09438b.htm.

Graham, Henry G. (1997). *Where We Got the Bible*. San Diego, CA: Catholic Answers.

Irenaeus. (AD 189). *Against Heresies*.

Johnson, Donald. (Producer). (2015). *Convinced* [Video]. Huntington Beach, CA: Runaway Planet Pictures.

Justin Martyr. (AD 153-155). *First Apology*.

Laux, Fr. John, M.A. (1990). *Mass and the Sacraments: The Mass, Seven Sacraments, Indulgences, Sacramentals. A Course in Religion*. Charlotte, NC: TAN Books.

Madrid, Patrick. (2001). *Where is That in the Bible?* Huntington, IN: Our Sunday Visitor.

Martin Luther. (n.d.). In *Catholic Encyclopedia* online. Retrieved from http://www.catholic.org/encyclopedia/view.php?id=7288

McCain, Paul T. (Ed.). (2007). *Concordia: The Lutheran Confessions-A Reader's Edition of the Book of Concord* (2nd ed.). St. Louis, MO: Concordia Publishing House.

Miravalle, Mark. (2014). *Meet Your Mother*. Sycamore, IL: Lighthouse Catholic Media.

Nasuti, Friar Nicola OFM conv. (2010). *A Neverending Mass: The Eucharistic Miracle of Lanciano*. Abruzzo, Italy: Ente SMEL.

O'Rahilly, Ronan, and Muller, Fabiola. (1996). *Human Embryology & Teratology*. (2nd ed.). New York: Wiley-Liss.

Pope Paul VI. (1965). *Dei Verbum*. Retrieved from http://www.vatican.va/archive/hist_councils/ii_vatican_council/documents/vat-ii_const_19651118_dei-verbum_en.html

Reformation. (2003). In *Merriam-Webster's Collegiate Dictionary* online. Retrieved from http://www.merriam-webster.com/dictionary/reformation

Ryland, Fr. Ray. (n.d.). "How Can We Respond to the 'call no man father' question?" Retrieved from http://www.catholic.com/quickquestions/how-can-we-respond-to-the-call-no-man-father-question

Rose, Devin. (2016). *Navigating the Tiber: How to Help Your Friends and Family Journey Toward the Catholic Faith*. San Diego, CA: Catholic Answers Press.

Saunders, Fr. William. (1994, September 15). "Protestant and Catholic Bibles." *The Arlington Catholic Herald*.

Schaetzel, Shane. (2013). *Catholicism for Protestants*. Amazon CreateSpace: Ozark Catholic Books.

Shea, Mark. (2013). *By What Authority?* San Francisco, CA: Ignatius Press, Lighthouse Catholic Media.

Sheen, Fulton. "Peter, Vicar of Christ." Retrieved from https://www.youtube.com/watch?v=Kqk--wvfZRo

Sippo, A., Donahue, T., Bonocore, M., & Hugh. "Did the Catholic Church forbid Bible reading?" Retrieved from http://catholicbridge.com/catholic/did_the_catholic_church_forbid_bible_reading.php

Staples, Tim. (2007, January). According to Scripture. *This Rock*, 18(1).

St. Justin Martyr. (n.d.). The First Apology. In *New Advent* online. Retrieved from http://www.newadvent.org/fathers/0126.htm

Trigilio, Fr. John. (2007, May 28). Catholic Q&A "Porneia and Moichao." Retrieved from http://www.ewtn.com/v/experts/showmessage.asp?number=503501

Thigpen, Paul. (2007). "Are You Saved?" Huntington, IN: Our Sunday Visitor.

Whitehead, Kenneth D. (1996). "How Did the Catholic Church Get Her Name?" Retrieved from www.ewtn.com/faith/teachings/churb3.htm

Waterworth, J. (Ed.). (1848). "The Council of Trent The Twenty-Fifth Session." Retrieved from https://history.hanover.edu/texts/trent/ct25.html

Wilhelm, J. (1907). Apostolic Succession. In *The Catholic Encyclopedia*. New York: Robert Appleton Company. Retrieved http://www.newadvent.org/cathen/01641a.htm

Suggested Reading List

As this book progressed, it became evident that we would never be able to fully address all the questions we might wish to answer. As we stated in the Introduction, our hope was to provide a springboard for further study. Therefore, we decided to provide these additional suggested resources.

Martin Luther and the Reformation

Adam, Karl. (2005). *Roots of the Reformation*. Zanesville, OH: Coming Home Resources.

Cole, Richard Glenn. (2013, September). "Martin Luther's Use of Rhetorical Masks for Jews, Princes, Clerics and other Enemies." *Journal of Religious History*, 37.

Luther, Martin. (1543). *On the Jews and Their Lies*. (Martin H. Bertram, Trans.). Kindle version (2008): Coleman Rydie.

Weidenkopf, Steve. (2015). "The Real Story of the Reformation" [CD set]. San Diego, CA: Catholic Answers Press.

Early Church History

Aquilina, Mike. (2008). *The Early Church*. New Haven, CT: Catholic Information Services.

Aquilina, Mike. (2013). *The Fathers of the Church* (3rd ed.). Huntington, IN: Our Sunday Visitor.

Bennett, Rod. (2015). *The Apostasy that Wasn't*. San Diego, CA: Catholic Answers Press.

Guarendi, Dr. Ray, & Fete, Rev. Kevin. (2010). *What Catholics Really Believe: Dispelling the Misrepresentations and Misunderstandings of Historic Christianity with Scripture and Tradition*. Novi, MI: Ninevehs Crossing.

Jurgens, William A. (1970). *The Faith of the Early Fathers, Volume 1*. Collegeville, MN: The Liturgical Press.

Jurgens, William A. (1979). *The Faith of the Early Fathers, Volume 2*. Collegeville, MN: The Liturgical Press.

Jurgens, William A. (1979). *The Faith of the Early Fathers, Volume 3*. Collegeville, MN: The Liturgical Press.

Moczar, Diane. (2010). *Seven Lies About Catholic History: Infamous Myths About the Church's Past and How to Answer Them*. Charlotte, NC: Tan Books.

Radice, Betty. (Ed.). (1987). *Early Christian Writings*. (Andrew Louth & Maxwell Staniforth, Trans.). London, UK: Penguin Classics.

Schonburn, Cristoph Cardinal. (2004). *God Sent His Son*. San Francisco, CA: Ignatius Press.

Shrek, Alan. (1987). *Compact History of the Catholic Church*. Ann Arbor, MI: Servant Books.

Authority of the Church

All the Popes from Saint Peter to Francis. (2013). Rome, Italy: Lozzi Roma s.a.s.

McKenzie, John L., S.J. (1966). *Authority in the Church.* Kansas City, MO: Sheed and Ward, Inc.

Shea, Mark. (2013). *By What Authority? An Evangelical Discovers Catholic Tradition.* (abbr. ed.). San Francisco, CA: Ignatius Press, Lighthouse Catholic Media.

Sheen, Fulton. "Peter, Vicar of Christ." YouTube. Retrieved from https://www.youtube.com/watch?v=Kqk--wvfZRo

The Bible

Graham, Henry G. (1997). *Where We Got the Bible.* San Diego, CA: Catholic Answers Press. (Original work published 1911)

Mary

Hahn, Scott. (2001). *Hail, Holy Queen: The Mother of God in the Word of God.* New York, NY: Image Books, Doubleday.

Miravalle, Mark. (2014). *Meet Your Mother: A Brief Introduction to Mary.* Sycamore, IL: Lighthouse Catholic Media.

Neubert, Fr. Emile, SM. (2010). *Devotion to Mary.* New Bedford, MA: Academy of the Immaculate.

Payesko, Robert. (1998). *The Truth About Mary: A Scriptural Introduction to the Mother of Jesus for Bible-Believing Christians*. Santa Barbara, CA: Queenship Publishing Company.

Evangelization

Hahn, Scott and Kimberly. (1993). *Rome, Sweet Home: Our Journey Toward Catholicism*. San Francisco, CA: Ignatius Press.

Nevins, Albert J., M.M. (1990). *Answering a Fundamentalist*. Huntington, IN: Our Sunday Visitor, Inc.

Rose, Devin. (2016). *Navigating the Tiber: How to Help Your Friends and Family Journey Toward the Catholic Faith*. San Diego, CA: Catholic Answers Press.

Catholics Considering a Return to the Church

Catholic Bridge. http://www.catholicbridge.com/catholic/

The Coming Home Network. http://www.chnetwork.org/

Those Considering Catholicism

Altemose, Sister Charlene, MSC. (1989). *Why Do Catholics...? A Guide to Catholic Belief and Practice*. Dubuque, IA: Brown-Roa, A Division of Harcourt, Brace & Company.

Coren, Michael. (2011). *Why Catholics are Right*. Toronto, ONT: McClelland & Stewart.

Madrid, Patrick. (2006). *Surprised by Truth: 11 Converts Give the Biblical and Historical Reasons for Becoming Catholic*. Dallas, TX: Basilica Press.

Ray, Stephen K. (1997). *Crossing the Tiber: Evangelical Protestants Discover the Historical Church*. (abbr. ed.). San Francisco, CA: Ignatius Press.

Rose, Devin. (2014). *The Protestant's Dilemma: How the Reformation's Shocking Consequences Point to the Truth of Catholicism*. San Diego, CA: Catholic Answers Press.

Schaetzel, Shane. (2013). *Catholicism for Protestants*. Seattle, WA: Create Space, Amazon.

Pro-Life

Horn, Trent. (2014). *Persuasive Pro-Life: How to Talk About Our Culture's Toughest Issue*. San Diego, CA: Catholic Answers Press.

Morana, Janet. (2013). *Recall Abortion: Ending the Abortion Industry's Exploitation of Women*. Charlotte, NC: Saint Benedict Press.

Pavone, Fr. Frank A., M.E.V. (2006). *Ending Abortion, Not Just Fighting It*. Totowa, NJ: Catholic Book Publishing Corporation.

Other General Information

Akin, James. (1999). *Mass Confusion: The Do's and Don'ts of Catholic Worship*. San Diego, CA: Catholic Answers.

Akin, James. www.jimmyakin.com

Bunson, Matthew. (2001). *The Catholic Almanac's Guide to the Church*. Huntington, IN: Our Sunday Visitor.

Cruz, Joan Carrol. (1977). *The Incorruptibles: A Study of the Incorruption of the Bodies of Various Catholic Saints and Beati*. Rockford, IL: Tan Books and Publishers, Inc.

Connell, Francis J., Chapman, Thomas A., & Sharock, David. (2011). *The New Confraternity Edition Revised Baltimore Catechism and Mass No. 3*. Whitefish, MT: Literary Licensing, LLC.

Hahn, Scott. (2016). *The Creed: Professing the Faith Through the Ages*. Steubenville, OH: Emmaus Road Publishing.

About the Authors

Roger Salstrom, Ph.D., was raised as a Methodist and spent most of his adult years as a Protestant. In 2010, after many conversations with his son-in-law Nick and after reading Scott and Kimberly Hahn's *Rome, Sweet Home*, Roger began to consider Catholicism in a new light. He was struck by

Scott Hahn's statement that his friend and pastor, Gerry Matatics, said there was not one Catholic teaching that was contradicted in Holy Scripture (Hahn, 1993, p. 65). This set Roger on a journey of discovery, culminating after four years with his entering the Catholic Church in 2015. Roger is currently Dean of the School of Business at a local university in Northern California.

Karen Salstrom grew up in the years surrounding Vatican II. She left the Church for nearly 40 years, spending her time in a variety of Protestant denominations where she picked up false information about the Church's teachings. After reading *Rome, Sweet Home*, Karen was convinced by the truth about Catholicism. Consequently, she sought to be reconciled to the Church. Since her return, she devotes much of her time to learning about the faith she never truly knew in her earlier years. Karen is a singer-songwriter, pro-life advocate, and owner of Holy Veils by Karen, making chapel and First Holy Eucharist veils for women and girls.

Roger and Karen met during their years as Protestants. They have been married since 1989 and have six children and ten grandchildren. Their journey to Catholicism has enriched their love for each other and for Christ.

About Leonine Publishers

Leonine Publishers LLC makes fine Catholic literature available to Catholics throughout the English-speaking world. Leonine Publishers offers an innovative "hybrid" approach to book publication that helps authors as well as readers. Please visit our web site at www.leoninepublishers. com to learn more about us. Browse our online bookstore to find more solid Catholic titles to uplift, challenge, and inspire.

Our patron and namesake is Pope Leo XIII, a prudent, yet uncompromising pope during the stormy years at the close of the 19th century. Please join us as we ask his intercession for our family of readers and authors.

Do you have a book inside you? Visit our web site today. Leonine Publishers accepts manuscripts from Catholic authors like you. If your book is selected for publication, you will have an active part in the production process. This book is an example of our growing selection of literature for the busy Catholic reader of the 21st century.

www.leoninepublishers.com